D0464158

Hauntings!

Hauntings!

Real-Life Encounters
with Troubled Spirits

(Original title: *True Hauntings: Spirits with a Purpose*)

Hazel M. Denning, Ph. D.

BARNES
&NOBLE
BOOKS
NEW YORK

This book is dedicated to

Burl Roy Denning

*my husband for forty-nine years,
who gave me love and support in
all of my endeavors.*

Acknowledgements

First I would like to express my deepest appreciation to the many people who, by sharing their experiences with me, made this book possible. It has been my great privilege to be a part of their lives, to witness their paranormal events, and to contribute in some measure to solving their problems.

Without the assistance of two psychically talented ladies this book would not have been possible. I thank Gloria Bell and Gail Ferguson for the many unselfish hours they devoted to this research. None of us were financially compensated for our time — it was a labor of love. All of us were dedicated to mitigating the pain and fear so many people experience during such paranormal events.

One dear friend, June Conway, who had been my first secretary in 1977, did the final proofing of the manuscript just before she died. It was a labor of love and I thank her posthumously. Three other people I would like to mention, Marge Montgomery, Connie Brooks, and Sylvia Alfred, were secretaries in the APRT office where I was Executive Director. They read my first chapters, and their enthusiasm and encouragement were strong factors in motivating me to complete the book.

Table of Contents

Author's Note

In order to protect the privacy of the individuals mentioned in these case studies, fictitious names have been used throughout this book.

Introduction

Many books have been written about haunted houses, but few present the material from the viewpoint of the spirit involved in the haunting. How do discarnates feel and think? Do they suffer? Does death automatically promote them to a paradise or, as some believe, to a hell?

During the 1970s I investigated many houses believed, by their owners, to be haunted. At that time I was active in the Parapsychology Association of Riverside, Inc. Many people who were experiencing strange and oftentimes frightening phenomena in their homes called us.

About that time I was doing research with one of the most skilled psychics I have known. Gertrude Hall's sensitivity to another dimension of consciousness was remarkable, and available on demand. Our work on haunted houses began when calls for assistance came to the Parapsychology Association. As president of the association I felt obligated to help people find a solution to their paranormal problems.

Our first experience working together on a haunted house convinced me that I had chosen the right colleague. Gertrude was so totally tuned in to any situation — the discarnates involved, the source of each problem — that the whole bizarre experience took on a new perspective and actually seemed normal. The entities with whom she conversed became living, thinking, feeling individuals — human beings in all respects save one: they did not have a physical form in which to function.

For a number of years we responded to many requests for help. When Gertrude's husband experienced a job-related transfer and she left California I decided my "ghostbusting" days were over. However, in the meantime I had worked for five years with another very gifted psychic. When the first call for help came after Gertrude's departure, I asked Freda if she would be interested in exploring her skills with haunted houses. She immediately agreed, and collaborated with me over a period of two or three years.

Throughout the intervening years I have often thought I would like to write a book about our experiences. As I saw it, one benefit in writing such a book would be to help people realize that there is no such thing as death; that life in the non-physical dimension is very real, very human, often very painful; and that there are very specific reasons why discarnates remain in our dimension.

A second benefit resulting from our efforts provided additional motivation for our work. We found that many of the discarnates were trapped in an interim space from which they could not escape. Some did not realize that they were "dead." Many were afraid to leave the safety of their physical environment because they believed that they would go to a place of punishment for their misdeeds. In almost all cases we were able to liberate these entities from their earthly entrapment.

Public response to the idea of haunted houses, possession, and communication with spirits of departed loved ones has changed considerably in recent years. A number of books have been written by individuals possessing academic credibility established through their work in physics, medicine, psychology, education, and the social sciences. This does not by any means imply that there is general acceptance of such subjects. The traditional scientific community is still discrediting all evidence of any reality beyond the physical.

However, the evidence of another dimension of consciousness is so overwhelming that I am encouraged to share my experiences with the many who are ready to listen. Following each of my lectures, dozens of individuals share their long-kept family secrets, assuring me that they have never told another soul about the "goings-on" after Uncle Ned or Aunt Helen "passed on." What a pity that such experiences, which could be a comfort to the bereaved, have remained so long a hidden part of our culture, their significance unrecognized as a normal part of our relationships, now and hereafter.

As I thought about it and reviewed the years spent in investigating this field, I was impressed with the vast scope of knowledge contained in those experiences and the life-changing effect of that knowledge. That other dimension took on a reality just as valid and normal as the physical world in which we all live. I realized that my experiences had actually left me with a firm conviction of that reality, and I no longer had any fear of death.

I had originally planned to exclude possession and psychic attack from this book. However, this phenomenon has become so prevalent in our society, and so much pain and suffering results from this type of invasion into human affairs, that I have decided it must be included in any examination of hauntings.

There is a final purpose which motivates the writing of this book. I believe the human race is moving into a new era of enlightenment. Driven by an inner force toward a recognition of their true identity as spiritual beings, individuals are discovering, in a very real sense, their birthright. One has only to read, look, and listen to recognize that whole new concepts are emerging on the world scene, and old stereotypes and outmoded dogmas are being replaced by a new paradigm.

Globally, humanity is changing. From five-sensory (physical) personalities we are becoming multi-sensory beings, possessing awareness of our spiritual natures and the unlimited capacities which this implies. It is my hope that this volume will reduce many of the old crippling fears and provide a new rationale to replace centuries of superstition and limitation.

CHAPTER 1

Insights from the Past

Have you ever had an eerie feeling that something was in the room with you, even though you could not see anything? Or have you heard sounds that you could not identify? Perhaps your best friend told you she thought her house must be haunted, because sometimes things were moved around. Of course you told her that it was her imagination. Everyone knows there are no such things as ghosts.

What if our materialistic or so-called "scientific" explanation of bizarre occurrences is inadequate to account for all of the incontrovertible evidence? This book is about some of that incontrovertible evidence.

Since the dawn of history people have attempted to explain and understand strange phenomena that defy all reasonable explanations. Every culture has its myths about monsters, spirits, devils, and fairies, intended to explain events which do not conform to widely accepted physical laws.

I believe knowledge is power. When people have the facts about any situation or discipline, they will respond with their minds rather than with their emotions. At the present time most people have little if any knowledge about parapsychology. If they have a paranormal experience their normal reaction is fear. They have absolutely no realization that encounters similar to theirs have been experienced by millions of other people, and therefore they infer that something is very wrong with their minds.

Although this is a terrifying thought for anyone to face alone, most people are afraid to share it with anyone else.

In counseling clients who have had psychic experiences I have found that the most effective method for reducing fear is to provide evidence that their experience is a common occurrence, and does not indicate mental illness.

Since this book is about hauntings and psychic invasions, it is not necessary to present a detailed historical background for the following chapters. That would require a full volume. However, some background for those unfamiliar with psychic phenomena will add to the reader's understanding, acceptance, and enjoyment of the following chapters. Let the reader note that it has been the great minds in all cultures and in all ages who have researched, espoused, and written about the paranormal field.

As the scientific age emerged and burgeoned into the monolithic structure we know today, anything that could not be explained in the scientific, purely material model of the universe was declared to be nonexistent, and ignored. People who harbored a belief in anything extraterrestrial were labeled delusional or ignorant.

Fortunately, a considerable number of hardy souls persisted in exploring the evidence, elusive as it was, that pointed to a non-material dimension of reality. They had the powerful support of historical precedents. Almost every culture throughout human history has espoused a belief in survival and communication with discarnate beings.

Today, the latest research in many scientific fields, particularly in physics and medicine, is producing evidence of the existence of intelligent energy outside of a physical body. Sensitive instruments respond to a force field that leaves the body in the moments immediately following physical death. Similar instruments record voices that did not originate from living persons.

It might be of interest to note that Alexander Graham Bell, following his invention of the telephone, spent considerable time working on a device that would pick up spirit voices. He died before he had perfected his instrument, but he was convinced such a device was possible and would result in spirits being able to communicate with loved ones.

Continuing that line of research, a number of investigators have recorded purported spirit voices. Probably the most comprehensive study was the work done by Konstantin Raudive, Ph.D.

His voluminous work, entitled *Breakthrough: Amazing Experiment in Electronic Communication with the Dead,* was published in 1971 by Taplinger Publishing Co., New York. Due to the enormous amount of meticulous detail included, reading Raudive's book can be tedious, but the evidence for the authenticity of the communicators is difficult to refute. Many of the voices in his examples spoke in different languages, usually the native tongue of the relative they were addressing.

The human mind is far more sensitive than any instrument, however, and a highly developed clairvoyant can easily communicate telepathically with discarnates. This telepathic interchange, the source of most of our information about the dimension of spirit life, has been going on from time immemorial.

Humanity possesses a rich heritage of interdimensional communication. This experience has been so common throughout recorded history that one wonders how there can still be so much resistance to it. I recall a conversation I had with a famous obstetrician in Denver, Colorado. He told me it always amazed him that so few Christians believed what they professed, even though all were indoctrinated with the idea that human beings have a soul that lives on following physical death. As he served families experiencing death, he was impressed by how few actually believed their loved one continued to exist beyond the grave. He is one of the growing numbers of doctors who believe that a person is a spirit with a body, rather than a body with a spirit. Perhaps the saddest aspect of this disbelief is the terrified reaction of almost everyone who experiences the full impact of confronting a spirit manifestation.

The spirit, finding itself very much alive and well, is often greatly distressed by the anguish it observes in the loved one in mourning. With genuine love, the spirit reaches out to assure the grieving relative or friend of its well being. When the response to its presence is one of shock and terror, it immediately withdraws, disappointed that its efforts to comfort caused so much distress.

A case comes to mind which well illustrates this effort to ease the pain of a surviving spouse. One night a young woman was awakened after midnight by a strong presence in her room. As she looked about she saw her husband standing in the doorway of the room. He looked at her sadly and said, "I am sorry, dear, you will have to raise the children without me. I love you." His image faded and the room was empty, but she knew he had been killed.

The next morning she received the news from the government that her husband had been killed in action at exactly the time he had appeared in her room. As difficult as this event was for her, she was greatly comforted by his visit.

Experiences such as this are common, and have been reported in the literature of the paranormal for centuries. However, people who have such an experience are afraid to admit it for fear they will be labeled insane. The average person who hears the story, more often than not, believes the individual is delusional.

In the last one hundred years many individuals, as well as organizations such as the Parapsychology Foundation, have invested considerable sums of money and years of research in an effort to understand the many strange phenomena that indicate the extension of life beyond the termination of the physical body. In the late 1800s Prime Minister Gladstone of England made the statement that psychic phenomena constitute the most important field of study a person can investigate.

In 1882 the Royal Society for Psychical Research was organized in England. Very shortly thereafter, in 1885, the American Society for Psychical Research had its beginning under the leadership of W. F. Barrett, an Englishman visiting the United States. These two organizations have played a significant role throughout the last century in the investigation of the entire field of the paranormal. In the early years, much of their attention was directed to communication with departed loved ones. Many of the most famous mediums of the time, including Mrs. L. E. Piper, Stainton Moses, D. D. Home, and Florence Cook, cooperated with investigators, and over a period of years produced volumes of cases indicative of bona fide contacts with intelligent spirits of former human beings.

While it must be admitted that some of the early mediums perpetrated fraudulent seances on a gullible public, under rigidly controlled conditions they also produced phenomena that indicated communication with spirit beings. Following the work of famous early investigators such as William Barrett, Richard Hodgson, Edmund Gurney, Professor Henry Sidgwick, F.H.W. Myers and others, paranormal investigators changed the emphasis of their studies from seances to the many other extrasensory abilities of the mind, such as telepathy, clairvoyance, precognition, and psychokinesis. An interest in communication with discarnate beings has also continued throughout this past century, primarily through organized spiritualist churches.

Unfortunately, the fraud connected with a large portion of seances, and the purported contacts with dead relatives, have so discredited the whole idea of spirit communication that even genuine manifestations are suspect. However, spontaneous cases continue unabated and are reported in various periodicals. Spiritualist churches enjoy a continued following. The old-fashioned medium has been replaced by channelers who, it seems, are springing up like proverbial mushrooms. One of the finest current books on this subject is *Chanelling: Investigations on Receiving Information from Paranormal Sources*, published in 1987 by Jeremy P. Tarcher in Los Angeles. The author, Jon Klimo, is a highly gifted psychic and channel. In his book, Klimo does an excellent job of relating the historical background of spirit communication. He takes the mysterious glamour out of the subject, and realistically delineates the dangers and pitfalls awaiting individuals who relinquish their minds and wills to an entity outside of themselves.

No amount of debunking and skepticism can negate the fact that people do see spirit forms, hear messages, feel physical contacts, and experience out-of-body trips. However, some of the explanations given for these experiences may be inadequate or faulty. Given our present knowledge of energy and the creative powers of the mind, it is possible that the person's mind actually creates some of the phenomena, even though they seem to originate outside of the individual involved. There seems to be substantial evidence for believing that certain negative states of mind existing in individuals attract paranormal activity. Whether the mind of the individual actually creates phenomena such as poltergeist manifestations, or attracts intelligent beings outside of the self who are responsible for the activity, is an important question. Perhaps the answer is that both are possible.

Our knowledge about the strange phenomena that are daily occurrences in all cultures must be said to be limited at best, and probably faulty in many respects. However, in some areas we have fairly good evidence for belief. At the present time much research is under way regarding near-death experiences, or NDEs. Many people report experiences that occurred while they were clinically dead, experiences that are significantly similar. These people report that they will never fear death again because they know they cannot die. They were totally aware and lucid while out of their bodies. In one such case, a lady reported seeing what the doctors and nurses did and said while they were working over her "dead" body, despite the fact that, in her physical body, she was blind.

Another area of strong evidence for survival of the soul concerns the large numbers of children who report knowledge of previous lives in considerable detail. These children often include information that they could not have acquired in their present lives. Are they picking up this information psychically, by tuning into other minds around them? Because of the nature of many of these reports, this does not seem logical. One such incident is reported in detail in an excellent book on past-life recalls. A boy insisted he had lived in a certain midwestern town, and had been killed on his bicycle when he was fourteen years old. He wanted to go and see his family again, and was finally taken to that town. He led the investigators to the spot where he had been killed, then to the house where he had lived. He knew the correct names of all the people in the house and they corroborated his entire story.

This is by no means an isolated case. Hundreds of such cases have been uncovered by researchers and reported in many volumes. In one case in India a murder was solved and the murderer convicted on the information furnished by a child who recognized him after she was reborn.

We like to think that we live in an enlightened age, yet superstition and fear still control the thinking of vast numbers of people. Unfortunately, higher education and intelligence do not always produce rational thinking. Fear and greed dominate the belief systems of many people. One world-famous scientist declared that he would not accept the paranormal field no matter how much evidence was produced. He had the good grace to add, "I realize this is a prejudiced point of view."

Academic degrees do not guarantee an unprejudiced examination of evidence in any field, whether it be religion, physics, medicine, education, or any other. In the field of parapsychology, for example, neither the epistemological nor the ontological assumption in science can account for the phenomena. Therefore the traditional scientist cannot accept any of the evidence as valid. Individuals who claim to see spirits, communicate with discarnates, travel out of their physical bodies, hear voices, or die and return with information about their experience, are diagnosed as mentally deranged and out of touch with reality.

I hope that the following chapters will mitigate the fears that plague many individuals who have had paranormal experiences and suffered rejection and even persecution for possessing the gift of higher sensitivity to the energies around them. If you are one of those fortunate people, regard your sensitivity as a blessing rather than a curse. Cultivate it for the dimension it can add to your life.

Many clients have come to my office for help following a psychic episode that involved anything from telepathy to an apparition. In numerous cases, they have been under the care of a traditional psychologist or psychiatrist who was treating them for delusions and even schizophrenia. In one such case the lady experienced telepathic communication with a troubled friend in another state. She awakened in the middle of the night in hysterics. Her husband soon calmed her, and convinced her that it had been a nightmare. Later, after she communicated with her friend and learned that the friend had herself been hysterical at that same time, she was terrified and consulted a psychologist. She believed that there was something wrong with her mind. Her therapist convinced her that she did indeed need therapy to get her mind straightened out. After three months with this therapist she began to question her progress and, hearing about our Parapsychology Association, called us. As miraculous as it may sound, an hour and a half on the phone totally allayed her fears. She terminated her therapy and, through reading, became involved in a personal study of telepathy and other paranormal abilities.

Often clients have told me they were afraid to tell their psychotherapist about certain experiences because they knew the response would be disbelief and a misdiagnosis of their problem. When I answer the phone it is not uncommon to hear a voice pleading with me to listen and not hang up until I have heard the story. Usually it is one of poltergeist activity, or of the appearance of "dead" relatives.

Many investigators in the paranormal field were once total disbelievers. Many of them set out to disprove claims made by psychics and other researchers. The evidence they uncovered was undeniable, and so convincing that they became dedicated to sharing their insights with others. The famous Dr. Gardner Murphy, director of research at the Menninger Foundation, once stated in the *Los Angeles Times* that anyone who did not accept the validity of paranormal activity was either ignorant or prejudiced, since the evidence was incontrovertible.

Let us briefly explore the rationale of the metaphysical field. The dictionary states that metaphysics is highly abstract and difficult to understand. It is the philosophical study of the true nature of the universe. Metaphysics tries to explain reality and knowledge.

Philosophy as it is presented in universities and colleges attempts to be scientific and so has lost its original purpose. Has science ever answered some of the most profound questions that plague thinkers of all ages? For example, is making a decision a physical or a chemical process? What is the nature and composition of intention, or purpose? What exactly are emotions? What is consciousness? The definitions we have come up with in psychology do not explain its nature; they only describe how it is manifested. When I was a student at the University of California, one of my psychology classes concerned the study of personality. At the end of the semester the students had memorized a number of definitions, but no one could successfully define personality.

Consider the findings of doctors working with multiple personalities. In this particular affliction the individual manifests a personality for a time and then, for no apparent reason, becomes another personality. Frequently the two personalities have no awareness of one another, and neither personality can recollect the activities of the other. If, for example, one personality has diabetes, there is no evidence of diabetes when the other personality takes over the body. The significance of this has profound implications. How can the same body be healthy as one personality and ill as the other? There would seem to be only one explanation — the body is subject to the mind. This has been the contention of metaphysicians for centuries and is currently promoted by transpersonal proponents who believe that the mind has a life beyond that which appears in individual persons.

If the mind then is independent of the body, it seems logical that it can operate independently of the physical vehicle. If that is true, then all paranormal manifestations can be logically explained as the expression of creative intelligent energies in or out of physical vehicles. Communication between minds should be normal rather than abnormal, whether or not those minds are confined to a body.

The capacities of the mind are the subject of considerable investigation at the present time. Dr. Stanislav Grof has spent three decades in research on non-ordinary states of consciousness. With a prestigious background, including an Assistant Professorship of psychiatry at Johns Hopkins University School of Medicine, he challenges the existing neurophysiological models of the brain and proposes a new model of the human psyche.

Dr. Roger J. Woolger, a Jungian psychotherapist and graduate of Oxford University, struggled through his disbelief in past lives and, after eleven years of working with this technique in therapy with his clients, has written of his experiences. He states, "Whole new dimensions of therapy were hinted at here and with them a complete revisioning of the origins of mental illness and the very nature of personality."[1]

The Association for Past-life Research and Therapies, Inc. has a world-wide membership of almost a thousand therapists who use their special technique to find the causes of physical as well as emotional illness. The results of this therapy are so spectacular that many believe it is the best evidence we have of the continuance of the life force. I was invited to speak in Japan and in India and report on the past-life regression work being done in the United States. Since belief in reincarnation is so much a part of these cultures, they consider our work to be significant verification of their beliefs.

It is estimated that well over half of the world's population believes in reincarnation. It is significant to note that it has never been the ignorant or uneducated who have espoused this belief. Starting with the ancients, Aristotle, Pythagoras, Socrates, Plato, Zoroaster, Mohammed, and Jesus all believed in reincarnation. How did they pay for having superior knowledge? Pythagoras was burned to death by a mob of illiterates, Socrates was sentenced to death on trumped-up charges, Zoroaster was killed by a spear in the back while he knelt at prayer, Mohammed was killed by poison, and Jesus was executed for teaching the brotherhood of humankind.

Through the centuries we find that some of the most famous of the early church fathers believed in continual rebirths, including St. Augustine, St. Anastaslus, St. Jerome, Origin, Synesius, Clement of Alexandria, St. Gregory, and two popes who were killed under Justinian's rule because they would not relinquish their belief. Reincarnation was removed from the tenets of the church at an Ecumenical Conference in Constantinople in the 1550s.

As for the Jewish religion, Rabbi Elias confirms a belief in rebirth and Rabbi Manassa ben Israel writes: "The belief or the doctrine of the transmigration of souls is a firm and infallible dogma accepted by the whole assemblage of our church..."[2]

Coming closer to our time, Schopenhauer once said, "Europe is that part of the world which is haunted by the incredible illusion that man was created out of nothing, and that his present birth is his first entrance into life."[3] Voltaire wrote, "Everything in nature is resurrection, and it is not more surprising to be born twice than once."[4]

Some of the great writers and poets who accepted reincarnation included Robert Burns, Ralph Waldo Emerson, Amos Alcott, Charles Dickens, Walt Whitman, Henry David Thoreau, Goethe, Kant, Longfellow, Whittier, Lowell, Mark Twain, Jack London, Edgar Allen Poe, and Nietsche, who wrote, "The theory of Reincarnation is a turning point in the history of man."[5]

Among the statesmen who shared this belief were the Earl of Balfour, Prime Minister Gladstone, Prime Minister William Lyon King, Frederick the Great, Napoleon, Lindberg, George Washington, Abraham Lincoln and Benjamin Franklin. Mr. Franklin penned my favorite statement: "Recognizing that I have lived many times before, I shall look forward to my next edition, hoping that the errata of the last shall be corrected in the next."[6]

In more modern times, believers included Henry Ford, General George S. Patton, Glen Ford, Ernest Wilson, Hans Holzer, Jess Stearns, Ruth Montgomery, Gina Cerminara, Arthur Ford, Bishop Pike, Leslie Weatherhead, Raynor Johnson, Dr. Carl A. Wickland, and Mohandas K. Ghandi.

Interviewers find that most professional theater people have a ghost story to report or a psychic experience to recount. Since theater people tend to be individuals with highly sensitive temperaments, as a group they are likely to have a great awareness of the energies around them. I shall not include any names here; some of these individuals are prominent in the public eye and frequently request that their names not be used in order to avoid ridicule. However, Danton Walker wrote two interesting books about this particular population in our society, and included the names of a few famous people who gave permission to be identified. *I Believe in Ghosts*, published in New York in 1969 by Taplinger Publishing Co., is a re-edited version of Walker's original *Spooks Deluxe*, published in 1956 by Danton Watts, Inc.

For a number of years the motion picture industry has very subtly introduced the public to paranormal phenomena. Although done under the guise of comedy and entertainment, this has gradually inculcated in the public mind the possibility of some validity to the material presented.

"Topper" was one of the first popular paranormal series, followed by "Bewitched." Both still enjoy periodic revivals. "One

Step Beyond" ran as a documentary; the producers guaranteed that the cases were taken from the actual experiences of the characters.

Numerous full-length films have been highly successful, starring such famous actors as Spencer Tracey, James Stewart, and Redd Foxx. One of the most recent productions, *Ghost*, received unprecedented public response, which amazed even the producers.

I believe most people want to believe in survival, and in the reality of contact with loved ones. The problem is it cannot be proven; perhaps it never will be. As one of my college professors said to me, "If the evidence we have were in any other field, I would have to accept it because it is so overwhelming, but in this (field) I cannot accept it." Who knows, perhaps the very preponderance of the evidence will eventually overcome the skepticism. In the meantime each of us must evaluate the evidence and draw our own conclusions.

Technical spirit communication is addressed in detail in chapter 12. I mention it briefly here as further evidence that interaction between the physical and spiritual world is highly beneficial to the whole human race. It should not be feared, but encouraged. A few of the benefits we have today came from inventors and investigators who apparently received specific information from a source outside of their own minds. The formula for making steel was given in a dream to Bessemer by an Egyptian metal worker. One of the great discoveries in the scientific world was the benzene ring; the discoverer, Kekule, credits a spirit informant. The scholar who deciphered cuneiform writing reported that a turbaned man whispered the key to him in a dream. George Washington Carver and Thomas Edison both credit an outside source for their inventions, or more accurately, their discoveries.

It has always been my contention that each person should have the right to his or her own beliefs. I firmly believe that we have no right to try to change or coerce another, nor to judge others in any way. My purpose in writing this book is not to convert anyone to any particular philosophy. I do know that many people have frightening experiences which they cannot understand and which have a detrimental effect on their lives. It is for these people, and others who are interested, that I have attempted to present evidence for a belief system which will make sense out of paranormal encounters,whatever form they may take. For readers who wish to pursue further evidence, in more detail, a bibliography is included at the end of this book.

In the following chapters the case histories reported represent some of the many reasons and purposes spirits have for remaining in the earth's energy field.

Chapter 2 deals with spirits or entities who are earthbound, so-called because they cannot escape the earth's vibration. They are trapped because of certain types of trauma that accompanied their deaths, and because of the memories carried over from past physical experiences.

---

1. Dr. Roger J. Woolger, *Other Lives, Other Selves* (New York: Dolphin Books, 1987), 21.
2. Joseph Head and S. L. Cranston, ed., *Reincarnation in World Thought* (New York: Julian Press, 1967), 92.
3. Eva Martin, ed., *Reincarnation: The Ring of Return* (New Hyde Park, NY: University Books, 1963), 133.
4. Walter Cronk, *The Golden Light* (Los Angeles: Devorss & Co., 1964), 96.
5. Manly P. Hall, *Reincarnation: Cycle of Necessity* (Los Angeles: The Philosophical Research Society, 1967), 104.
6. Ibid., 108.

Death Traumas Entrap Some Entities

A First Encounter with a Discarnate

My very first personal encounter with a haunted house was with my own home. I must confess it was a terrifying experience. I was in my twenties and my explorations into the paranormal were only beginning. I had no real knowledge of this field, but I had a driving desire to investigate it.

My husband had gone to a banker's convention and I was alone with our baby son for a week. On the third night I awoke about 3:00 in the morning and I knew without a shadow of a doubt that I was not alone. I immediately thought of a burglar and very cautiously opened my eyes. The street lamps outside my window illuminated the room well enough to allow me to see objects with a fair amount of clarity. I saw nothing unusual. Slowly I turned my head to take in the entire room. Nothing was there except the furniture, but that very real and "heavy" feeling of a presence persisted. I recall vividly feeling the hair rise on my scalp, and goose bumps erupt on my arms. I confess to a feeling of sheer terror and total helplessness. I grabbed the covers and pulled them up over my head. Nothing happened. My shaking gradually subsided and I fell asleep.

The same experience was repeated the next night, with the same reactions, only not quite as intense. I called a friend who had

13

a little experience with the paranormal and described the events of the previous two nights. She allayed my fears considerably by telling me that someone had probably died traumatically in that house, and did not know how to leave or where to go. This "someone" was earthbound and wanted help. My friend assured me that I was in no danger. She did, however, tell me to demand that the entity leave my house, and to say it firmly.

I wasted no time in inquiring about the previous occupants of the house. I discovered that a woman had suffered pneumonia and died of strangulation in the front bedroom. It was at this point that I put together a number of strange incidents that had occurred over a period of months prior to my night visitation. Our front door had a heavy Yale lock which made a loud clunking sound when it was released. I had heard that sound on a number of occasions and thought it must be my imagination, for there was never anyone near the door when it occurred. Two or three articles had fallen off shelves for no apparent reason,. The most baffling event, however, involved my husband's tennis racket, which was stored at the very back of a shelf, leaning against the wall. If it had fallen as a result of the house shaking, it would have fallen forward and remained on the shelf, lying flat, as the shelf was very wide. What puzzled me was that the tennis racket had tumbled to the floor. I remembered studying the fallen racket and wondering how it could have gotten there.

Other strange noises caught my attention from time to time, but they had made me more curious than frightened. Following my night visitor, I put all of these events together and decided that something was going on that was not normal. I had one uneventful night and then was awakened a third time by this overwhelming sense of a presence. I sat bolt upright in bed. In as firm a voice as I could manage I said, "This is MY house, you have no right to be here, so get the hell OUT, NOW, and don't come back." I sat there in the bed, waiting for something to happen. It could have been my imagination, but I had the very real impression that the atmosphere in my room changed and the oppressive feeling lifted almost instantly. Now I would explain it as a negative energy leaving the room. At that time we were not talking about energies, and I had no knowledge of how to help souls who were caught in their last environment.

Trapped in Fear

Years later, after considerable experience in the field, I received a phone call at 5:30 in the morning. A young woman in a nearby town literally begged for my help. She said she was going crazy because she was terrified of dying. Voices were screaming in her head; she had tried but she could not stop them. I made an appointment with her for 2:30 that afternoon. Around 8:00 A.M. she called again and begged me to see her sooner. She said she could not endure the pain any longer. I told her to come at 9:30. I called my psychic colleague Gertrude, and asked her to come at once. I had a feeling I was going to need her.

When the woman and her husband arrived, he had to help her into the house. Her whole body was quivering ; she was unable to relax and stop the shaking. The first thing Gertrude said to her was, "You have not been in that house very long, have you?" After this was confirmed Gertrude went on, "The grandmother died there and the family moved away. The grandmother stayed in the house. She is very angry, and feels frightened and abandoned. She does not know what to do to find her family."

The young woman began to relax as she answered Gertrude's questions. She asked why the old woman was attacking her so violently. Gertrude explained that because she was very sensitive, she was picking up the thoughts of the grandmother. In other words, she was experiencing the fear and pain of the old woman. Gertrude went on to explain that the old woman had always feared death and could not accept her own. When she found herself unable to communicate with anyone and her family gone, she became insane with fear and rage.

The events of the past few days were reviewed and explained. One event of particular interest involved an old rocker in the bedroom. The young woman asked why she felt such overwhelming discomfort when she sat in it by the window, although if she moved it to another part of the room she was comfortable. Gertrude explained that the grandmother had occupied that room and her favorite place to sit was in a chair by that window. She was angry when anyone else sat in that spot, because in her dimension she was still sitting there. She felt displaced and uncomfortable trying to occupy the same space as a human form.

Within a matter of twenty minutes our client was calm and rational and quite comfortable with our explanation. Her fears had, of course, been part of the problem, and once she understood what was happening she was no longer afraid. But then as she sat talking she said, "I have a terrible headache." I showed her three techniques to relieve the headache but none of them had any effect. Then in a direct, firm voice Gertrude asked, "When were you beheaded?" The response was immediate and dramatic, "Not once but twice. They botched it the first time and had to do it again."

The discussion which followed cleared up a number of things for this client. She was a college graduate with a very responsible position in the corporate world. She had refused to accept her psychic ability, which had manifested itself many times throughout her life. She attributed this attitude to a desire to be acceptable to her colleagues. As we discussed her lifelong struggle not to be "different," she realized that her chronic headaches were a determined effort to "keep the lid on" her psychic ability. We discussed the beheading episode and she "saw" that it was punishment for being a healer in France. At that time she had vowed never to use her gift again. The terrific pain in her head ended as soon as she admitted the purpose of it. A follow-up two years later found her still free of headaches.

Needless to say, we psychically contacted the grandmother and helped her to understand that she was "dead" but that, as she had discovered, there was no such thing as death, and she could go anyplace she wished to go. She, too, responded to Gertrude's concerned support and left the house, hopefully for a happier environment.

Brief Analysis of the Above

This experience contains a number of elements that give us insight into life here and beyond. The grandmother's inordinate fear of death, coupled with her rage, locked her in a veritable dungeon of horror from which she had no means of escape. It would have been interesting to have had a case history of that lady. Obviously, she lacked any religious beliefs that might have assisted her in the transition. From other cases we can deduce that she had considerable anger before she died. In such cases we repeatedly find that the individual harbored a great deal of guilt, as well as resentment and anger. Therefore they expect punishment of some sort in an imagined "hell" or similar place. Speaking to people and finding themselves ignored, experiencing physical bodies walking right through them, frustrated by their inability to get a response from people they once loved and knew, their minds do indeed approach a state of insanity. They may remain in that state for a very long time. This causes considerable distress to people near them who are sensitive or psychic and who pick up their very thoughts and feelings and accept those irrational responses as their own. A few studies in mental institutions have been successful in identifying patients who were not insane, merely responding to ideas and feelings which did not originate in their own minds.

Let us now analyze the experience of the psychic young woman. Although she was known to me, I had no knowledge of her physical or emotional problems until this dramatic encounter. For years she had mild experiences of a paranormal nature, which she always rationalized or denied. She had also suffered headaches for many years. She had joined the Parapsychology Association of Riverside, Inc. and admitted she had an interest in "that stuff," but totally denied that she had any psychic abilities.

Out of this encounter with the spirit of the grandmother she not only solved her headache problem, but uncovered the past-life event which was apparently the source of her fear of being psychic in the present. In the past-life regression process clients are frequently asked to get in touch with the last conscious thought they had before their spirit left their body in a previous life. There is strong evidence that the evaluation of the self at that moment just before death remains in the psyche somehow and is carried into the next or subsequent incarnations, manifesting often, from the moment of birth. For instance, people who die in a rage are born with rage which must be overcome. A common example is the individual who dies feeling worthless, or guilty. In the current life they experience a constant struggle for better self-image, for status, for acceptance. In the case we have just reviewed, the young woman died with a determination never to have or use psychic ability again. With an understanding of her own history and the purpose of it, she was able to accept that her pain had been the very factor that had forced her to seek help and achieve liberation. A five-year follow-up confirmed the success of that experience.

Many questions arise out of such encounters. Was the sequence of events purely accidental? Was the couple's choice of that haunted house an accident, or was destiny at work in some unidentifiable way to put that young woman where she would be forced to deal with her sensitivity? When the call for help came, I had no knowledge of the background of the haunted house. What convinced me to call for Gertrude's help? That was not my usual response when clients called for an appointment. Why, at the very moment when we had the client calm and accepting that her panic was no more than her picking up the entity's fears, did she suddenly develop a violent headache? And why, when she saw that it was because she had kept the "lid on" her psychic ability, did it immediately go away? How did Gertrude feel so sure of herself that she could ask, "When were you beheaded?" Answering that question brought about the final resolution of the young woman's whole problem — the denial of her sensitivity — and allowed her to accept her special psychic talents with no further conflict.

This may give the reader a very limited view of the dynamics of the investigative process, and to some extent support the hypothesis that nothing is accidental or purposeless. The facts we have been able to gather suggest that life is indeed purposeful on both planes of existence, and that some energy or intelligent power orchestrates the opus. With infinite finesse every individual's design complements the designs of his contemporaries with the precision of an intricate oriental textile. Evidence of the wisdom of this interconnection is almost never apparent. Who can be comfortable with the violent behavior of the masochist and the sadist? Yet there can be no question that each personality is meeting its own needs in the behavior of the other, painful as some of those behaviors may be.

A Friendly "Live-in" Spirit

I would like to share one more case of an entity trapped by its fear of leaving the familiar environment. We were called to a house in the Norco area by a lady who claimed that she had a "live-in" spirit. This spirit sat in the corner of the living room by the fireplace most of the time, but occasionally would cry through the teakettle. A number of her friends, when visiting her, asked if she had a baby in the house, for they heard the unmistakable sounds of crying. It always occurred when the teakettle reached the boiling point. Our hostess had no fear of the visitor, whom she felt was an elderly woman, but she was curious about its purpose in being in the house.

When we arrived at the house I set up my tape recorder. After numerous attempts I had to give up. The recorder would play forward and reverse, but it would not stay on "record." Our hostess brought out her recorder; it also refused to function on "record." Gertrude was amused. She explained that the entity was an elderly woman who resented our intrusion. At that point I took out the pad and pencil I always carried. The entity immediately became very upset and vocal — through Gertrude, of course. She indignantly asked what I was writing and stated that she did not want anyone writing about her. I told her I was sorry but I intended to make some notes, and I promised they would not hurt her in any way. When I asked her to give me her name she snapped, "That is none of your business."

She was very surprised that Gertrude was aware of her and could talk with her telepathically. She told us she was glad the lady who owned the house was not frightened by her and would let her stay, because she liked to sit by the fireplace. She was comfortable and safe there. When I explained to her that she could move on into her dimension and be much happier she became very defensive. She said she did not want to go anywhere else. I finally asked if she was afraid she would go to hell if she left. She reluctantly admitted she was afraid of something like that. We then assured her there was no such place, and told her she could be much happier if she moved higher into her dimension and asked for help.

We were able to identify her as an old lady who had lived in the neighborhood. Our hostess was surprised and gave us quite a history of her behavior in life. The woman had been a recluse; the children were all afraid of her, and she had erected a high wall around her yard to keep them out. She had no friends, only a few relatives who lived in other areas. Because of her unfriendly behavior she believed she was a bad person and expected to be punished when she died.

We talked with her for almost an hour, answering her questions and assuring her that she could have help and go to a happier place. At one point in the conversation our hostess explained that the spirit was welcome as long as she wanted to stay, as she was not uncomfortable having a spirit in her house. She said, "Sometimes I open the door for her when we go into another room." In an unexpectedly humorous response the spirit replied, "Does she think she has to open doors for me? I go right through doors."

She seemed very grateful and far less defensive and said she would consider our explanations. While we were still there, other spirits came into the room and assured her they could help her. She said she would go with them, and as far as we could tell, she departed. When she had gone, both of our tape recorders worked perfectly. Checking with the home owner a couple of weeks later, she reported no more signs of the spirit presence.

This was the first encounter in which we found evidence of a spirit fearing it would go to hell if it left the safe environment it was used to, but it was not the last. As we worked in this field, we found a number of spirits who remained because they felt safe, and feared what they would encounter if they left. In questioning them their fear always reflected guilt and the expectation of some sort of punishment.

A Young Stowaway

Ethel was quite sensitive, but had never thought of herself as being psychic. After borrowing a card table from her parents' home, she began to be aware of an invisible presence in her house, and she picked up fear energy. Puzzling over her feelings, she recalled that as she grew up in her parents' home she had experienced those same feelings. In retrospect, she connected them to the card table.

At about that same time her six-year-old son began to awaken in the night and cry out. When Ethel went to him he would insist he was hungry and wanted some food. Often she would make him a sandwich, but he never took more than one bite before going back to sleep. Although this behavior continued almost nightly for over a year, it never occurred to her that the card table might have any connection with her child's nightmares. She felt quite helpless, frustrated by his behavior and annoyed at never getting an undisturbed night's sleep.

In a casual conversation Ethel expressed her frustration over the son's nightmares. I suggested we try hypnosis to see if she could "pick up" his problem. She had been in one of my psi classes; I knew she was more psychic than she realized. Our first attempt was quite successful. She "saw" that there was a small male entity in her house who had died of malnutrition and starvation. Her son Gary, a very sensitive child, had unconsciously responded to the hunger feelings of the entity.

In the altered state of consciousness, she spoke with the boy entity. He had been born in England. Having lost his parents, he was unable to support himself. He decided to come to America and stowed away on a ship bound for the United States. Unable to get food from his hiding place on the ship, he became very ill and died. His spirit remained with the ship and was attracted to a man whose aura was kind and loving. This young man was on his way to America, where he intended to become a citizen of the United States and make his fortune. As time passed the man was successful in business, married, and became Ethel's father, Gary's grandfather.

We gleaned this much information from our first attempt to understand Gary's behavior. We were now determined to know more about the little spirit. Why had he remained earthbound for so many years? And what had any of this to do with the card table?

We decided to invite another psychic to join us. Perhaps we could learn more about this unusual cast of characters by using two psychics in an altered state. When we met there were six of us. Three friends who knew of the experiment insisted on being included, and since they were all believers and would not introduce a negative energy into the session, we welcomed them. The card table which Ethel had borrowed from her parents was set up in the middle of the room. She was quite convinced that it played a significant role in the phenomena.

Almost as soon as they were in a trance Ethel said, "The spirit is under the table."

Norma, the other psychic, agreed and added, "And he is very frightened. Why is he so frightened?"

In a surprised voice Ethel replied, "He isn't the only spirit here. There are about half a dozen others. They are all adult spirits and he is afraid of them."

Norma continued expressing what the two psychics were picking up. "They have been enjoying their control over this little spirit for years. That is why he hid behind or under the card table. When the table was brought over here, he came with it."

Ethel began a dialogue with the adult spirits. They were very belligerent, declaring they would not leave. Both psychics then explained to the spirits that they could find happiness if they would give up bickering among themselves and stop harassing the little spirit. It took about twenty minutes to persuade them to withdraw, with the understanding that if they did not find the freedom Ethel promised, they would be back.

Ethel now turned her attention to the little spirit. She told him he was now free and did not need to hide under the table any longer. She asked him to stop influencing her son at night. He was very apologetic and said he had not meant to harm anyone. He was happy to take her advice and ask for help from someone in his dimension. Both psychics reported that a very gentle spirit came into the room and took him in charge.

The only evidence we had for the validity of this experience was the fact that Gary never again cried out in the night to ask for something to eat. Ethel believed that the uncomfortable energy she had felt in her house was no longer there, and she was certain the vibrations she had so often sensed when she was close to the card table were also gone.

This experience was an introduction to a group of entities stuck in a power struggle. We have encountered this same phenomenon in a number of haunted houses through the years of our investigations. In each case there was one spirit who dominated the rest. The others were always subservient and afraid of the dominant entity. At times fights erupted when two entities struggled for control. The energy generated from such conflicts had the power to manifest physical sounds. This seemed to be the case in a large country house we were called to investigate. The family would be awakened during the night by loud sounds which seemed to be coming from the roof. They reported that it sounded like a fight going on over their heads. When she tuned in to them, Gertrude encountered almost a dozen entities. They were indeed angry, the majority terrified by the two most powerful leaders. It took both of us, using all our powers of persuasion, to convince them that they could better themselves by leaving. As far as we know they did leave, and the family reported no more unexplainable sounds in their house.

In the next chapter we will deal with an entirely different kind of entity. These spirits have a happy, positive energy and remain on the earth plane to help or serve those in need. Sometimes they have a prior connection to the people they help, but often they are attracted solely by the unhappy energy and pain they recognize in a living individual. They are not highly evolved spiritually, and often do not realize their potential, but they find satisfaction in serving those they find in need. In that service they further their own spiritual growth.

CHAPTER 3

Encounters with "Helping" Entities

The Case of Alicia

My firsthand introduction to mediumship came about in a most interesting way. My neighbor, Holly, came to my door one morning and asked if I would hypnotize her and help her find an article she had misplaced. I agreed, although this was the first time she and I had worked together in any kind of a client-therapist relationship. She assured me she was a good subject and thought she could easily accomplish her purpose. She was a highly intelligent middle-aged woman, well-educated, a community leader, and the wife of a prominent physician. She possessed one of the deepest masculine voices I had ever heard in a woman.

Imagine my surprise when I had not even reached five in counting her into the trance state before a high, childish voice said, "Hello, may I come in?"

What could I say but, "Of course, and who are you?"

"Oh, I am Alicia and I have not talked with Reba for a long time." We had a short visit and then she said gaily, "Well good-bye now, tell Reba hello for me," and she was gone.

My neighbor spontaneously came out of her trance state and looked at me with amazement. "What happened?" she asked.

"You tell me," I responded. "Someone by the name of Alicia claims she is a friend of yours."

Holly laughingly explained that fifteen years before this event she had worked as a medium, and Alicia had been her contact. When I asked about the name, since I knew her only as Holly, she told me that was a nickname. Her real name was Reba.

I was seriously intrigued by this experience and insisted on Holly telling me about her work as a medium. I knew too much about fake seances and the trappings of mediums who are charlatans to be taken in by them, so I had always avoided them and had never attended a seance. Now here was a medium right next door, and certainly the encounter I had just been through was no fake. The idea that I might do some personal investigation in this field was, to say the least, fascinating. I asked Holly if she would like to join a parapsychology study group I was leading and allow my students to experience mediumship first hand.

She was delighted with the idea and invited us to meet in her house for the next session. Thus began a series of meetings that gave me a vast amount of evidential material and added one of the most fascinating cases to my own research.

One of Alicia's favorite contributions to the meetings was to go around the group, which usually consisted of about ten people, and give each person a quick psychic reading, or answer questions. I was particularly intrigued with the amount of knowledge an entity can pick up on people in the physical dimension. Often, however, her information did not make sense to her, because it came in symbols. For example, she told one lady she saw a canoe by her. The lady laughed and explained that her father had taught her from early childhood that she must always paddle her own canoe.

Alicia lived in Holly's house with her, so in one sense hers was a haunted house. However, we finally did get around to the reason Alicia attached herself to that environment. She had died of starvation when she was seventeen, during the Civil War. Holly's psychic ability had attracted her in the first place and then, finding that Holly was a very unhappy person, Alicia had remained in an effort to comfort her. When I explained to Alicia that it was in her best interests to move on in her dimension and not be earthbound, she said she had to stay to help Holly when she got depressed. At that time Holly's husband was terminally ill and she was nursing him at home. He was a large, heavy man; nursing him was a difficult task. In addition, he was demanding and had a bad temper.

Holly told me that sometimes, when she was feeling really unhappy, she would get a strange feeling in her solar plexus, like a tickle. She would have to laugh in spite of herself, and then she felt better. Apparently Alicia's efforts were not in vain.

This was not a case of possession in any sense of the word. Alicia never invaded Holly's personality, with the possible exception of the brief times when she took over Holly's voice and spoke to us through her, always with Holly's full consent and cooperation. Following her husband's death Holly took a trip east to visit some friends. The night she left we had a meeting in her home. She planned to start the trip after the meeting, preferring to drive at night. Alicia became very impatient over the delay and told us she had been waiting in the car for hours and wanted to leave. When she returned home, Holly told us that Alicia had been a great help on the trip and had "told" her when to go and when to delay. She had missed two bad storms and a hurricane by heeding Alicia's warnings. Again Alicia reminded us that she could not leave because Holly needed her. At one of the meetings, however, she did report to me that she had taken my advice and was now improving herself— she was taking piano lessons. She was a happy little spirit, always cheerful and quite pleased with herself because she was helping someone. I use the word "spirit" advisedly since one evening I had laughingly called her a cheerful little sprite. In an indignant voice she responded, "I am NOT a sprite, I am a spirit."

One very amusing incident clearly illustrates the humanness of some entities. Holly had asked me to tape one of the sessions so that she could hear Alicia, since she was totally unconscious during the time Alicia used her voice. I set up the tape recorder, and when Alicia announced that she was ready, I reached down to turn it on. In a surprised and frightened voice she spoke, and the following discussion ensued.

"Hey, what's that thing? I'm getting out of here."

"No, no, wait a minute, that is just a tape recorder."

"What's a tape recorder?"

"It is an instrument that makes a record of your voice so Holly can hear you. She has never heard you speak."

"Will it hurt me?"

"No, of course not."

"Will it hurt Holly?"

"No, it does not hurt anyone. It is just a machine that makes a record of your voice."

"Well, all right, if you are sure."

All went well, and we had an interesting meeting. At the end I reached down to turn it off and Alicia said, "Wait a minute, are you going to play it? I want to hear it." I replied that I would be glad to play it for her, to which she responded, "Wait a minute, I want to get a friend." We all laughed but waited and in a few seconds her voice came through again, "All right, we're back now, you can play it."

One day Holly told me Alicia had finally left. The class had terminated, and Holly had worked through some of her problems so that her life was much happier. She described her experience as a warm, happy completion. She had been watching television, and suddenly the screen became clouded and she was aware of a figure in a lovely southern dress with full, hooped skirts between herself and the screen. It remained there for a few seconds only and Holly had the mental impression that it was Alicia saying good-bye. To my knowledge she never returned.

A Spirit Helper

A friend in her early eighties became a client when she called me and asked if I could help her with her Parkinson's disease. For two years I went to her home once a week for two or three hours and worked with her using past-life therapy. She arrested the disease; for a number of years it did not progress, but we were never able to cure it. During therapy she once said that her shaking was an unconscious expression of her rage. It was certainly true that she would not let go of the anger she carried against two people in her life. All of my efforts to help her forgive them were of no avail. She would verbalize forgiveness, but the emotion would crop up again when she was in a trance, and she was not able to face whatever it was that caused such a strong rage.

At any rate, we both felt our efforts were productive, since she did not, as the doctor had expected, get worse. When we worked she could remain for a number of minutes without a trace of the quivering that is a common symptom of Parkinson's disease.

I describe all of this as background for some very interesting paranormal experiences.

The first incident involved her favorite violet plant. The violet began to die, and all of her efforts to save it proved ineffective. Finally she talked to it. She promised that if it would recover and bloom again, she would stop wishing to die and go on with her writing. The change was almost miraculous. In a very short time the violet not only recovered totally, but grew into a very large plant with the most beautiful cluster of purple blossoms I have ever seen. My friend was overjoyed and resumed writing articles, a number of which were published.

Another experience began with a minor annoyance. My friend found it difficult to reach down and turn on the heater in her bathroom. One day she was thinking about the problem, feeling sorry for herself because there was no one to help her. When she went into the bathroom to take her bath, the heater was on. She was astonished, for she knew she had not touched it. She had been to the bathroom a number of times since her last bath and the heater had been off. Being somewhat psychic, she thanked "whoever" might be helping her. After that she found the heater on a number of times when she went in to take a bath. There was no doubt in her mind that she was being aided by an unseen helper. In fact, she confessed to me that she often sensed a presence in her house. It was a great comfort to her because she felt protected.

A Helper with a Sense of Humor

A young lady called me one day to announce that she had a haunted house, and since she had heard I was interested in such "things" she wondered if I would like to investigate it. Her story describing the incidents leading up to her call was indeed unusual. The first time she was aware of the presence, a small vase left a shelf and moved through the air a few feet in slow motion. It landed gently on the floor, undamaged. Next, her clothes dryer door opened in her presence, just at the moment the cycle for drying was completed. This occurred a number of times. One day, when her husband was home with a bad case of flu, a friend came in to visit her. She excused herself and explained that she had to take him his medicine. As she walked down the hall to his room, carrying a glass of water in one hand and the medicine in the other, she was about to ask her friend to open the door for her, but as she approached it the door opened by no visible means. This delighted her because she had a witness to the phenomenon.

Her husband totally refused to accept any of her stories and insisted she was imagining things. One day she and her husband were having lunch. Their three-year-old daughter was sitting in her high chair drinking milk through a straw. The father teasingly took the straw and put it in his glass. The child started to cry and whimpered, "I want my straw back." The straw floated up from his glass, moved across the intervening space and settled back down in her glass.

Her husband's response was instantaneous and violent. He banged the table with his fist and shouted, "It didn't happen! Don't ever mention this again! Don't you ever tell anyone about this, it never happened!" However, the experience made her very happy. Now she had proof positive that she was not imagining things, and of course she had to share it with all of her friends.

Gertrude engaged in a dialogue with the visiting entity. The entity said she was a relative of the young mother, and very fond of her. Since the mother was unusually psychic, it was fun to be around her and play these games. She explained that she would leave eventually, and that she knew she was free to go whenever she wished. She enjoyed helping the young woman, who was aware of her, appreciated her, recognized her as a person, and was not afraid of her.

When we called for a report a few months later, the spirit had departed. This case poses some interesting questions. Since the young mother was unusually gifted psychically, did she unconsciously control these manifestations with her own kinetic energy? This would seem quite possible in the case of the door opening because she needed to get through, but in the case of the vase moving through the air, it is not so feasible. There would be no reason for her to even think of performing such a trick.

On the other hand, if it is possible that our minds are powerful enough to control matter, which is a claim now being made by many researchers, it is quite logical that her mind unconsciously controlled these manifestations, since her psychic powers were highly developed. The fact that she was unaware of her own abilities is beside the point. Many people do not recognize their own paranormal powers.

Another explanation, the most common one, recognizes another dimension of existence and is therefore much more interesting to the average individual. If the activity in that house was controlled by an entity of intelligence in the other dimension, did she use the kinetic energy of the young woman in the house to perform her physical feats? This is the claim of many investigators, as well as one explanation for the entities themselves when they seem to communicate through a sensitive. Alternatively, can a discarnate generate its own energy to create physical manifestations without the help of a physical person in the environment? Perhaps all of these explanations are valid. There could be more than one way for an entity to project its presence into the physical world.

While the reports of a psychic investigator are certainly not proof of such phenomena, they must be given some credence. Many of these reports can be checked and verified. In all of the hauntings I have investigated, my psychic colleague has apparently carried on a natural and very human dialogue with the discarnate, and much of the information forthcoming has been accurate. Therefore, the entity hypothesis for hauntings seems to be supported by considerable evidence.

Relatives Who Remain to Help

Many tales are reported about relatives who remain in the environment to be near and assist their family of origin. Two cases come to mind which I feel are authentic. I know the families well and can vouch for their integrity. The entities in both cases were purportedly maiden aunts (called in that period "old maids") who had lived with the family and served the family for their "keep." They were not treated as servants, but their lives were devoted to household chores: cooking, washing, ironing and so on.

Following their physical deaths these women continued to serve the family. Their presence seemed to manifest most often in the kitchen, where they would turn off fires to prevent food from burning. Often they would remove bread or cakes from the oven and set them out on the counter at exactly the right time, frequently when the cook was slow about her responsibility. Occasionally beds which had been left unmade would be neatly turned up.

In almost all such cases the psychic activity occurs when no one is present. Seldom are such manifestations observed. It is not uncommon for furniture to be rearranged in a matter of seconds, silently, but rarely does it occur in the presence of a human being. A famous case in point was Matthew Manning, the gifted English psychic whose living room furniture was frequently overturned and moved while the family was out of the room only a few minutes. Having heard no sound while in another part of the house, they would return to the living room and find it totally disarranged.

In one of the cases cited above the entity was especially active and obvious in her manifestations. She claimed to be the sister of the lady of the house and had no wish to move on to other dimensions until her sister could go with her. According to our psychic communication she was happy staying in the home she had occupied for so many years. She enjoyed being with her family, even though they could not talk with each other any longer. She felt their love and found happiness in continuing to serve them from her dimension, often preventing burned and overcooked food.

Many people believe in a guardian angel. From the reports of psychics we can assume that many of these entities are the souls of people who have loved us and wish to continue protecting us. They are not in the same category as "lost" or "earthbound" spirits. They are free to come and go, to enjoy the freedom of their dimension. Part of that freedom gives them the privilege of "helping" those they love, often protecting them from dangers in the physical world. The literature is replete with stories of such intervention.

One very dramatic incident comes to mind. A mother glanced out of the window to check on her little son who was playing in the yard. To her horror she saw him run into the street to retrieve his ball. Just as he stepped off the curb, his body lifted into the air right in front of a car and was gently deposited on the curb. She raced down the stairs and into the yard to grab the child and hold him to her breast. He looked at her wide-eyed and said, "Mommy, somebody picked me up and put me back in the yard." In relating this incident to a psychic friend she was told that the invisible rescuer was the child's grandmother, who had recently died. Can we prove that? Of course not. As with many of the paranormal manifestations which are so common, we only know what happens. At this point in time we cannot prove any of the explanations. In all probability there is no single answer, and all of our speculations may have some validity.

The following case illustrates the behavior of spirits who remain attached to a house and want to be helpful to the occupants. They frequently stay in the building for many years and, if the occupants are sensitive, they manifest their presence. Less sensitive individuals never know the spirits are there. A very famous obstetrician who lives and practices in the Midwest told me this story about his home.

He and his wife had a real fondness for old houses. When they discovered this particular one, they both felt it was waiting for them to move in. It required considerable repair and modernizing, so they hired a contractor to make the necessary changes. Over a period of several weeks the contractor found it difficult to keep men on the job, particularly the electricians. One of the men finally told him there was something funny going on in the house and the men were scared. They would put new wiring in and the switches would go off and on when no one was near them. On other occasions the workman would turn off a switch, walk away, and the switch would go on again behind his back. Tools would be moved, doors opened and shut with no visible explanation. In spite of these difficulties the job was eventually completed and the doctor and his wife moved in.

One of the first manifestations of their "live-in" spirit occurred when the doctor sat down to smoke a cigarette. His lighter was on the coffee table in front of him. As he reached for it, the lighter glided along the coffee table, out of his reach. He jokingly told his wife that someone was trying to tell him to stop smoking, and since the message came from an invisible source he had decided to heed it. So he stopped smoking.

One day, while his wife was sitting by the window knitting, the sky became cloudy. Because her husband was in the room, she said out loud, "I guess I should get up and raise the shade." The words were no sooner out of her mouth when the shade, on its old-fashioned roller, was raised to its maximum opening.

The two of them were delighted to have this unusual house with its playful and helpful energies. They made no attempt to discover the identities of their uninvited guests. At the time the doctor told me about them they were still performing small services and making their presence known. He thought there were two entities, but he was not sure. They never did anything destructive or harmful and they provided an unusual subject for conversation when friends and relatives came to visit.

In the next chapter we will explore experiences with entities who are earthbound as a result of guilt. This is one of the most common problems earthbound spirits have to deal with. Although many of them remain in that state of mental torment for long periods of time, there is a way out of their dilemma.

CHAPTER 4

Guilt-Ridden Entities

A Trio in Crime

The following case brought us considerable satisfaction because it resulted in more documentation than most cases provide. The names and dates that we first obtained psychically were later found in the historical society of Pasadena and in the cemetery. A complete skeleton and a gun were discovered bricked up in the fireplace during the remodeling of the house. Because it is a long and involved case, I shall begin at the beginning.

Mrs. Louise Brooks called me and asked for our help. She said she was not afraid, only curious; why were spirits living in her house? She had confronted the real estate people who sold her the house. They told her that two previous owners had disappeared, supposedly out of fear, without even claiming their equity.

The house was a three-story red brick mansion almost one hundred years old. No one had lived in it for a number of years. Mrs. Brooks loved old houses and was delighted to be the owner. She planned to remodel the house and move in with her family: her husband, who was a college professor, and their three children. While the house was being remodeled they visited it frequently. Almost from the first visit she began noticing strange events. Mrs. Brooks was psychic. Not only could she feel the presences, she also "knew" that there were three entities, a woman and two men. They often found the doors and windows open when they went to the house, even though they were certain they had carefully locked them on their previous visits. They also found things moved or rearranged, certainly not as the family had left them.

One day she took a friend to see her new home. As they walked through the house, the friend tried to open one of the doors, which seemed to be stuck. The friend looked terrified and said, "This house is haunted. If you move here I shall never come to visit you."

Mr. Brooks was a complete skeptic and laughed at his wife's claims. However, it was his habit to go to the old house to correct papers or study in order to get away from the noise of the children playing. One day as he sat on the davenport he heard a scraping sound coming from the kitchen. He looked up to see a dish moving along the sink. When it was opposite him it moved toward the edge of the sink. He braced himself for a crash, but the dish stopped just short of falling off. He went home and described his experience. In a frustrated and unbelieving voice he said, "Okay, okay, so we have a haunted house. Now what do we do?"

It was at this point that Mrs. Brooks heard about us and called for our help. We drove over and she took us to the house. As we walked through the downstairs, Gertrude picked up no energy in any of the rooms. We went upstairs and through the hall. Gertrude looked through the doors of the first two rooms. As Mrs. Brooks and I discussed the events of the past few weeks Gertrude walked ahead of us. Suddenly Gertrude disappeared through the door of the third room. It happened so quickly I was surprised, and followed her into the room. She told me later that it was as if someone had grabbed her and pulled her in. Mrs. Brooks followed me, of course, so that all three of us were in the room. Gertrude spoke with the three spirits, and from her words I could gather fairly well what was being said.

The spirits told her to get those people out of the house. It was their house. I tried to explain to them that the Brooks family had purchased the house, so now it was their house. I said, "Since you do not have a body they do not know you are here," to which they indignantly replied, "We do too have bodies." Gertrude asked them to do something so that I would have some evidence of their presence. Suddenly my right arm was lifted up at a right angle to my body. When I tried to put it down, it was held firmly at that level. I said, "Okay, you have proved your presence, you can let go now." My arm remained in midair, so I just went on talking with my arm suspended. After three or four minutes the support was removed and my arm fell to my side.

As I stood there, I was aware of intense heat ; perspiration was running down my back. I was surprised because I knew I was not afraid or nervous and I could not understand the cause of my perspiration. Later I learned that the other two women also perspired profusely during our conversation with the entities. Mrs. Brooks told us that ever since she bought the house, that room had always been hot. Her daughter wanted the room for her own, but she too was uncomfortable in it because of the temperature. As strange as it seemed, when they opened the window of that room no breeze came through, even when there was a breeze in other rooms.

We talked with the three spirits for about half an hour, explaining how they could be free of the house and move on to a happier place in their dimension. I told them that if they really liked the house so much, they could construct one exactly like it in their world. They were very skeptical, and asked if they could stay until they had checked out our claims. Mrs. Brooks told them they could stay as long as they wished.

The story that finally unfolded was truly bizarre. The three spirits had been "living" in that house for about thirty years. The woman, Doris, and one of the men, Edmund, were brother and sister. They were the last of the original family that had owned the house. They had lived in it together until Doris and her boyfriend, Richard, became engaged. Edmund, furious with his sister, killed Richard and buried him behind the fireplace so the crime would not be discovered. When Doris and Edmund died within a short time of each other, the three spirits found themselves still together in the old house.

We talked with them and assured them that they would have help if they would just ask for it. They said they would like help but they were afraid, particularly as they expected some sort of punishment because of Edmund's crime and their involvement in it. I asked for help for them, and Gertrude told me that three more spirits had come into the room. For a time the six of them conversed. Gertrude assured me that the new arrivals were explaining the situation and promising help to Doris, Edmund and Richard. But those three insisted they wanted some time to check it all out, so we all agreed they could take as much time as they needed to investigate the truth of what we were telling them.

We terminated our first visit and drove home. When Gertrude arrived at her house the three spirits were there. She asked them why they had followed her home, and indignantly told them to go back where they came from. They told her that they had not been able to talk to anyone before. No one had ever listened to them, so they had a number of questions they wanted her to answer for them. She said she would give them fifteen minutes for their questions; then they must leave. They agreed, and proceeded to ask her to explain some of the problems that were bothering them. She conversed with them for the fifteen minutes and then told them they would have to leave, and they did.

Three days later Mrs. Brooks called and told us that the three occupants of her house had departed. They had contacted her psychically and asked her to come before 4:00 P.M. that day because they were going to leave and they wanted to say good-bye. She could not make it at that time; when she reached the house around 5:00 they were no longer there. The room they had occupied was cool and comfortable. When she opened the window the breeze blew through it. Although she thanked us, it was obvious that she was disappointed. She had rather enjoyed having a haunted house and I think she would have been pleased if the spirits had stayed.

As I explained earlier, the names of Doris and Edmund were found in both the cemetery and the historical society records, and Richard's (presumably) remains were found when the house was remodeled and the fireplace torn out. The remains had been hidden, along with a rifle, behind an extra wall of bricks.

We contacted Mrs. Brooks some months later. The house was finished and the family had moved in. The youngest daughter was delighted with the room of her choice because it was light and airy. There had been no more evidence of any spirit visitors.

Double Trouble

One of our longest and most difficult cases required almost three months to resolve. Prior to our involvement, a spiritualist minister and a Protestant minister had been called by the family. The Protestant minister, after hearing the story, refused to have anything more to do with the family and asked them to leave his church. He accused them of Satanism and told them they were the Devil's henchmen. The spiritualist minister was aware of the entity and attempted to communicate with him. When she tried to exorcise him by calling on God to banish him, he forced her to the old wood stove and tried to push her arm down onto the hot surface. With the help of the others she was able to move away from the stove. She ran screaming from the house and refused to return. We later learned that the entity had burned the arms of the woman he lived with in that house, by forcing them against the stove, and that in the end he had probably killed her.

The family first became aware of the entities (it turned out there were two of them, a man and a woman), when they left the house well-locked and returned to find it open. Clara and Lawrence Brown had purchased the old house because they enjoyed remodeling old buildings. After finding their house open a few times, Lawrence used large screws to fasten the windows shut. When they returned the screws were on the floor under the window.

One day a neighbor came in to visit. As she and Clara sat talking, the lampshade on the table slowly made a complete turn, paused, then turned back to its original position. The neighbor, quite frightened, left abruptly. Clara then saw a face floating over her mantle, but when she approached it the face disappeared. When Clara told one of her other neighbors about the incident, this neighbor produced a snapshot of four men and asked if any of them looked familiar. Clara immediately identified one of the men — it was his face she had seen over her mantel. According to the neighbor, that man had died in the house shortly before she and her husband bought it.

One night Lawrence was awakened by the screams of his wife. She lay in the bed beside him, her arms twisted around her neck and her legs bent back, unable to straighten out her body. His efforts to "untangle" her were fruitless until he became very angry, swore at whatever was responsible for hurting his wife, and demanded that she be released. Almost instantly her body relaxed and she was all right, although considerably shaken and frightened. A few nights later he heard the piano playing. His wife was not in bed. Knowing that she could not play the piano, he was puzzled. He got out of bed and went into the living room, where he found Clara playing gospel hymns. His presence interrupted her; she stopped playing and returned to bed. Later it was learned that the lady who had lived in the house was a spiritualist minister and often played hymns when she held meetings there.

Lawrence awoke a few nights later to find his wife gone again. Going to look for her, he found her walking across the living room floor, slightly bent over, her hand out as if she was holding a cane, drooling from the corner of her mouth. She was walking with a slight limp. When she saw Lawrence she demanded, in a masculine voice, that he get her some beer and cheese. He was able to talk her back to her normal self and to bed. The neighbors later revealed that the man who had lived in the house often went to the corner grocery store and returned with beer and cheese, which he consumed while sitting in an old chair in his yard.

When we made our first visit to the house, some of the above events had already occurred. Gertrude had a very clear and open conversation with the entity, who said his name was Harry. When I asked him how he managed to do so many physical things, he said he had been an inventor in his life, so when he went into the other dimension he simply experimented with energy until he learned how to control it on the physical plane. On our first visit we were unable to persuade him to leave. He told us flatly that he did not believe a word we were telling him. He loved Clara and had no intention of leaving her. When we asked why he harassed the Browns so much, he said he was angry because they were changing his house all around. He liked it the way he had it; he did not like what they were doing to it. Since he would not leave, we told the Browns that we would bring another psychic with us on our next visit. Perhaps she and Gertrude could talk Harry into terminating his occupation of their home. We spent considerable time with Clara, attempting to allay her fears. She was so terrified at this point that her fears were increasing his power over her. As time went on she realized that when she could control her fear the manifestations lessened.

A few days after our first visit we received another call from the Browns. When we arrived, seven frightened people were sitting in their living room, waiting for us. One of the men said, "I didn't used to believe in ghosts, but this sure has made a believer out of me." Then they described what had happened the night before.

They had been discussing the phenomena in that same room when Clara's brother walked through the door in a very inebriated state. Waving his arms in the air he said, "So you think you have ghosts in this house, huh? Well, I don't believe in such damn nonsense. There ain't no such thing as ghosts."

They all declared they heard the same thing. Out of the air had come the words, "So you don't believe in me. I'll damn well show you I'm here." With that the brother was knocked to the floor and dragged about eight feet to the door of a bedroom. He disappeared through the door, which slammed shut behind him. Lawrence tried and failed to open the door. Two other men tried, without success. Finally two of them, pulling together, were able to open the door. The brother was lying on the floor, frightened but unhurt.

Our conversation with Harry was not very productive on this visit. He was quite surly and continued to call us fools. He insisted that we would be unable to do anything about it if he didn't want to leave. The other psychic I had brought along was no help at all. She was convinced that he was of the devil, as she put it, and she was so frightened she would not return to the house under any conditions. That was fine with us. Her fear didn't add anything constructive to what we were trying to do. We did appeal to Harry's interest in Clara, telling him that if he really loved her as he claimed he would not hurt her or interfere with her sleep as he had been doing. He promised he would not hurt her again, but insisted he had no intention of leaving the house. He kept his promise. No more unpleasant night episodes occurred.

A new attempt to reach Clara now manifested. When she was on the telephone he would take over the line and speak to her. This happened a number of times. When she called to tell me about it, he broke into our conversation and laughed. I never did hear him speak, but the laugh was unmistakable, definitely not her voice. She told me that when he spoke it was not conversational, in sentences, but rather in isolated words.

We advised the Browns to play down their experiences rather than talk about them, for we were well aware of the harassment that can come to families in this situation. They did not take our advice. Before long cars were constantly cruising past their house, and people peeking in the windows. News reporters frequently knocked on their door, demanding interviews. The story finally reached the *National Inquirer*. Clara and Lawrence decided they could not endure having their life constantly disrupted. Regretfully, they decided to move. We told them Harry would follow them, but they hoped we were wrong and moved to another town.

Before they left we had another session with Harry at their house. He was very defensive. He told Gertrude that he would not leave under any circumstances and that we could not make him. I explained to him that he was using energy to manifest. I would bring ten psychics to the house and generate so much energy that he would be forced to leave. Impressed that I meant business, he promised that if I would not do that he would discontinue his harassment of the family. He said he was not ready to leave Clara, that he loved her, but that he would not do anything more to make her uncomfortable. We all agreed to this arrangement. A follow-up much later in their new home assured us that he had kept his promise, although Clara told us that she was still aware of his presence.

This case provided my only experience of being propositioned to cooperate with an entity. Harry promised me that if I would let him remain and make no further attempts to get rid of him, he would go with me and make things move at my command when I gave lectures to groups. In other words, with his help I could appear to control physical matter. I flatly and firmly told him, "No deal," but I could not help wondering if anyone ever actually worked with entities in this manner.

One other example of his influence involved a neighbor who lived across the street from him. In life he and she had been good friends and had often visited one another. Although much younger than Harry, she basked in his appreciation of her musical talents. A composer of songs, she hoped to get rich by selling them to some popular singing group. From what we could learn, Harry had not been very popular. He had few friends; most people considered him a sour old man. His young neighbor, however, was quite psychic and had some communication with him after he died. He told her he would see to it that a certain one of her songs was published. To further that end, he told her where to send it.

When she followed his advice, the song was accepted. Many months later she told me that it had earned approximately $30,000 in royalties. She also gave me a copy of the tape. For the life of me I could not understand how that song had become so popular, or why it remained on the best seller list for a number of weeks. But then I am not a fancier of rock music.

In order to understand how such experiences are possible, and why some people are so traumatized by influences from another dimension, it is important to examine some of the dynamics involved. It had been my experience that all such phenomena were attracted by the victims. The energies that attracted psychic manifestations were usually anger, rage, and resentment. These emotions are highly charged with destructive energy, and attract entities who are earthbound because of their own uncontrolled rage.

Clara and Lawrence seemed to be a compatible couple. They were certainly supportive of each other in their mutual problem, and when we talked with them they seemed to love each other. However, I made a number of appointments to see Clara alone in order to help her cope with Harry's harassment. I know very little about palmistry, but I have studied it briefly, and on occasions when I need all the insight I can get, I will look at a hand. This was one of those occasions. I had never seen a hand that revealed so much conflict in relationships as Clara's did. When I asked her about her childhood I learned that her father had beaten her frequently because she would not "mind." The reason was obvious to read in her hand. Her life line and her love line were widely separated under the index finger, which is a sure sign of an independent individual. In addition, the two major lines were crisscrossed with many fine lines. The pattern resembled a web, as if the smaller lines were trying to bring the two major lines together. This indicated a major battle in Clara's life. She needed to be her own person, yet somehow handle the pressures and demands of her close relationships.

We spent considerable time exploring her conflicts with her father, in hopes of reducing the rage she still felt toward him. As a grown woman she recognized that she had been a difficult child to raise. Her father had honestly believed he had to control his stubborn child. She had married quite young to get away from home, and discovered to her distress that her husband was also a dominating male. They soon had three children. After that she felt she could not leave Lawrence and deprive the children of their father. Contrary to appearances, however, she was tremendously angry at him and felt trapped in the marriage. She had never realized that she was gifted psychically. Unusual things that happened in her life, like knowing about events before they occurred, seemed normal to her.

Here we had a perfect setting for psychic phenomena — an entity angry because his house was being remodeled, and a female who lived in a constant state of rage, feeling trapped, with no prospects for escape. Clara was really a very nice person, with a limited education but an excellent mind. She tried to be a good wife and mother and live up to what she considered her Christian principles.

As we met and worked at helping her find her own autonomy and self-worth, Clara began to change. It was very difficult for her to let go of her fear of Harry, but gradually her confidence in her ability to control her own situation increased. Without Clara's negative energy, Harry became less powerful. When he intruded she was able to tell him to "back off." He no longer had any power over her. We also had two or three sessions with both Clara and Lawrence. He was totally cooperative in trying to understand how he was hurting her. She reported that they were communicating at a much improved level of understanding. When they moved they both felt they were making a new beginning in their lives. We felt satisfied that Clara would no longer be anyone's doormat or scapegoat.

What happened to the female entity who had played the piano through Clara on two or three occasions? We had no other contact with her. We believed she was a spiritualist minister; Harry, by his own statement, was an atheist. According to one hypothesis, he might be expected to be earthbound while she would be free to move above the astral plane into a higher spiritual dimension. Why would she return to manifest through Clara in that one way? Any answer would be pure speculation.

Was the success of our work with Harry due to our convincing him that he had to leave Clara alone? Or was the diminution of the phenomena due to the empowerment of Clara? In all probability both factors combined to accomplish our purpose. The process assisted both Harry and Clara to evolve toward a greater understanding of their life purpose. Certainly Clara learned the destructive power of her anger, and worked conscientiously to rid herself of it. The most we could do for Harry was explain how he could be free of the earth plane. We left it to him to decide when he would take that step. We did have the satisfaction of seeing a major change in his attitude and receiving from him a guarded expression of appreciation for our concern for his welfare.

We closed this case with a feeling of satisfaction. It had been rough going some of the time, especially when we were called in the middle of the night, but we had learned much from the multitudinous aspects of the situation. Seldom does one case present so many facets of the phenomenon of haunting. It reinforced our belief in the power of rage to create havoc in the lives involved, and in the rehabilitating power of forgiveness and love when genuinely expressed, even between individuals on two different planes of existence.

In the next chapter we present three cases in which the entities remained on the earth plane because they were angry at a particular individual and wanted revenge. Cases of this nature are quite common and create tremendous problems later for the entities.

CHAPTER 5

Malevolent Entities

Three Angry Sisters

When Mrs. Brown called us for help her situation was desperate. She could no longer endure the persecution to which she was being subjected. She had been slapped, pushed, punched, and tripped. The day before she called us, she had been lifted into the air and thrown into the bathtub with such violence that her left arm was broken.

She was very frightened. She assured us that she had never been a coward, but this experience had overwhelmed her because she felt so helpless. She felt she had no defenses against this unseen, abusive force. She assured us that she was a good Christian woman and had lived a circumspect life. She prayed and attended church regularly and had always tried to practice the highest Christian principles: love, kindness, and honesty. She was quite ready to believe that, for some reason unknown to her, the Devil had it in for her and was persecuting her.

Mrs. Brown was a well-educated, attractive, middle-aged woman. Her demeanor demanded respect and attention. She was eminently qualified for the title "lady," and in spite of her emotional state, on our first visit to her home she served us tea from the family tea service. We chatted informally and I listened carefully for any clue that would give me some insight into her involvement in this experience. In the meantime Gertrude was "tuning in" to whatever energies might be present.

Entities often resent the presence of an investigator. They may leave altogether while the visitor is in the house, or withdraw into a corner or remote part of the dwelling until the investigator leaves. This behavior results from the entity's fear of being removed. When a family calls for help in such cases, the entity is completely aware of what is going on and often resents the interference. The degree of their apprehension depends upon their own spiritual understanding.

When we first arrived, Gertrude could not pick up the intruding energy. However, as we talked she became uncomfortably aware of two female entities who grew increasingly belligerent as Mrs. Brown described her life. First she talked about her deceased husband, and the metaphysical philosophy that had helped her handle his leaving her. Then, in answer to our questions, she talked about her childhood. I noted the anger in her voice as she described her two sisters, both older than her by a number of years. From her conversation I also deduced that her psychic harassment began shortly after the death of her two sisters. According to her description of their relationship, she and her sisters had quarreled constantly; they had hated one another as far back as she could remember. From her point of view her sisters had always been jealous of her. They made her life miserable as she was growing up, but she assured us that she had forgiven them after they died, and no longer held any hard feelings toward them.

At this point Gertrude was ready to report on what she was picking up. She told Mrs. Brown that both of her sisters were present and determined to make her life as miserable as they believed she had made theirs. At first she could not accept that they would reach back from the grave to harass her. As she talked, however, her deeply buried resentment came to the surface, and became so obvious that she herself recognized her real feelings. She admitted that she still carried a deep rage against her sisters. Because she had a good background in metaphysics, she was able to understand our analysis of the problem. We explained how her own anger made it possible for them to be drawn to her and manifest their presence so violently.

The transformation in her was an amazing thing to see. She looked at us with a shocked expression and said, "I can't believe I have been so blind. I have studied all this stuff for years and I know exactly what you are telling me, but I have never applied it to myself. How COULD I have been so unaware of what I was doing?" We assured her that deep emotions can be so completely buried we remain unaware of them until they manifest in such an unpleasant manner that we are forced to seek relief. Only then do we recognize and deal with the underlying problem. Even though she recognized her own role in the situation, Mrs. Brown remained confused about how she could be free of the two sisters. We explained that it was entirely in her hands. She had only to forgive herself and them and, with genuine love, send them on into their own dimension.

Mrs. Brown was almost euphoric. I must confess I had some skepticism over such a dramatic change in her attitude. She said she understood her sisters' jealousy. The entire family had showered her with attention and constant praise for her accomplishments and her beauty. This had happened because she was the last child and grandchild in the family, much younger than the others. She expressed remorse for having carried her anger so long, and asked her sisters to forgive her.

I expected her to need more help in handling her own anger, but in this case I was wrong. We left her in a very happy frame of mind, feeling that the whole matter had been cleared up. She was right. She had solved the problem as soon as she was made aware of her own negative role in her little drama. Because she had a background of years of spiritual studies, in this case it required only her insight to achieve the transformation. A follow-up found her very grateful for our help and totally free of the visitors.

Controversy over a Wall

As I mentioned earlier, my experiences had convinced me that no one was annoyed by entitics unless some attitude or emotional state of their own attracted this phenomenon. However, when I met Ann I decided I had found the exception to the rule. Ann was a beautiful woman in her late thirties, well-educated, the mother of two grown children, and apparently quite successful in a joint business with her husband. She proved to be a fluent conversationalist, and we talked about her haunted house as calmly as one would discuss the weather. Her attitude toward her husband and children indicated a deep love and pride in all of them, and there was nothing in her conversation that would give any hint of friction between her and her husband. My first appraisal was that she was a well-integrated, successful, reasonably happy wife and mother.

She and her husband had purchased a very attractive house with an extremely high, thick stone wall enclosing the entire front yard. This enclosure was landscaped with shrubs and beds of flowers, including a rose garden of unusual beauty. Both of them felt as if they lived in a fortress, and after they purchased the house they decided to remove the wall and share their lovely garden with neighbors and passersby. They hired a crew of workmen to remove the wall. Almost immediately, strange things began to happen. The men would find their tools apparently moved from one place to another. One worker insisted he had been pushed from behind and knocked to the ground, but when he looked around there was no one there. Removal of the rocks proved to be much more difficult than anticipated, and a number of injuries occurred to the workers. Two of them quit, giving no excuse but refusing to return to work.

In addition, Ann was uncomfortably aware of a presence which she could not see or identify, but which caused her to experience uncontrollable feelings of fear. She was totally objective in relating her feelings. She explained that she did not believe in ghosts, but that these experiences were certainly not normal and she was determined to find some explanation for them. She was not certain, but she believed objects in the house had been moved, and unidentifiable noises occurred almost daily. She rationalized these occurrences by questioning her own memory regarding the objects — perhaps she did not remember having moved them herself. The noises might be the result of the house settling, or maybe even rats in the wall. The feeling of a presence bothered her the most, since she felt she had no control over it. She was not comfortable with the thought that something outside of her had that much power over her.

As Ann and I talked, Gertrude excused herself and began walking through the house. She soon returned and reported that she had contacted the spirit, who was very angry with Ann. It seemed that this spirit and her husband had built the house to fulfill a lifelong dream. They were very private people and had built the wall to keep everyone out who was not specifically invited to visit them. Their visitors were few and far between. They did not like children and wanted to make certain that no "little monsters" invaded their property. This entity had spent many months planning and working in her yard to create the beautiful garden she wanted. She loved flowers much more than people. She had also planned the inside of her house with features peculiar to her taste in color and design.

She and her husband had a very short time to enjoy their dream house before they were both killed in a car accident. She had put so much of herself into the house that she could not leave it. After her death she had returned to enjoy her home from the other dimension, only to find that strangers had taken over the property and were tearing down her beloved wall and remodeling her house. Furious, she determined to make them as uncomfortable as possible. She had tried to stop the workmen from tearing down the wall but did not have enough power to do that. All she could do was stand by and see it demolished. She followed Ann around the house sending her as much anger as she could, wishing that she, too, would die. It was not surprising that Ann, even though she had never considered herself psychic, was reacting to this powerful negative energy.

Ann reacted positively to Gertrude's explanation. She was visibly relieved just to have an explanation, and she said she thought she could understand the entity's feelings. She apologized to the former owner and explained that she was sorry she had hurt her, but that the house was no longer her property and she must relinquish it. At this point it was our responsibility to help the disturbed entity. We explained that she was "dead," which at first she vehemently denied. Finally she acknowledged the truth of our words, since she could not refute the evidence we gave her that she no longer had a physical body. We explained how she could be happy by moving into her dimension and building another house there, which could be an exact replica of her earthly one if that was what she wanted.

She soon agreed to leave. Our request for someone to come and help her was answered and she left willingly with a spirit helper.

Ann enthusiastically expressed her gratitude, inviting us to visit her again. Since it was my practice to follow up on all of our cases, I went back to her home two weeks later. It was then that I learned more about her personal life.

There had been no sign of the entity following our visit, and she felt greatly relieved on that score, but as we talked she began to discuss her relationship with her husband. They had disagreed sharply on the remodeling, including the matter of the wall. He could see no reason to go to all that expense. In fact, he thought the wall might give them a privacy that would be rather pleasant.

As she talked about their relationship I began to be aware of a long-standing conflict between them. She told me that he nearly always disagreed with what she wanted. In their business, if she did not go along with his decisions he made her feel inadequate, even stupid. She had decided to remodel the house in order to have a project away from their business in which to express her own creative ideas. He had agreed when they bought the house, but when it came to the actual labor and what he considered an unnecessary expense, he changed his mind.

Ann was quite unhappy with her life. As we talked about it she acknowledged that her husband was not really a bad husband. He provided well for his family, never abused her physically, and could be very nice some of the time. All of their friends thought they had a really good marriage. I suggested that she might benefit from some therapy to improve her image of herself. She was well-educated and knew how to put on a good front, but underneath that polished exterior she was emotionally crippled, as many people are, by her own feelings of inadequacy.

We parted on a positive note, and she again expressed her gratitude. As I drove away, my thoughts centered around her anger and resentment. She was no exception to my earlier conclusion: where there are negative manifestations the object of the harassment frequently harbors emotional negativity, in the form of anger, resentment, fear, or guilt.

Relevant Analysis

Speculating on the significance of the dynamics in the above two cases, I think back to the many times I have heard my Christian friends ask the question, "Why does God allow or cause suffering?"

This concept, that God is responsible for humanity's suffering, has always struck me as a gross misunderstanding of the primary design and purpose of life. If we postulate the purpose of life on this planet to be spiritual evolvement, it follows logically that each soul and/or personality is responsible for its own acts and responses to life. All of the major religions teach that concept. The Master Jesus expressed it very simply but with powerful implications: "As you sow, so shall you reap."

During the many years that I have used Past-life Regression Therapy as a counseling tool, the concept that people are responsible for their own acts, behavior, and attitudes has been reinforced and substantiated thousands of times. We punish ourselves when we violate or act out of harmony with any Universal law. There are certain laws we cannot break without suffering painful consequences. A simple example on the physical plane is the law of gravity. If we fall off a roof we do not blame God because we are injured. We did not break the law of gravity. Having acted in a manner that is contrary to that law, we suffered the consequences. If we place a finger in fire and are burned, it is our own act that brings on the pain. Those laws are impartial, immutable, dependable, and operate in the non-physical dimension as well as in the physical world. If this were not so we would have a chaotic planet.

Through the years I have listened to thousands of clients in an altered state of mind describe their infractions of what we shall term "spiritual laws." They are always well-aware of how they have violated the sacred precepts by which people must live if human relationships are to be peaceful, harmonious, and happy.

Referring back to the two case histories cited above, both provide dramatic examples of the suffering caused by rage, resentment and guilt. Early in our investigations of haunted houses it became apparent that the two worlds, physical and non-physical, interact continuously in accordance with spiritual law. In the physical world, anger generates anger. Similarly, where there has been hate or rage between two people and one dies, that powerful negative energy continues to hold the two personalities locked into a painful relationship, until the problem between them is resolved in a way that dispels the negative energy. That unpleasant relationship may be expressed on two levels as in the above cases, or the two individuals may return to another physical life together.

In Past-life Regression Therapy this pattern emerges repeatedly. Many clients are locked into relationships with people they have abused in the past. According to their own insights they have returned with that individual to make amends. If the differences between the two are not resolved, conflict is inevitable. The relationship continues through as many life encounters as are necessary, until the lesson of forgiveness and love is finally learned.

All of the evidence in profane and religious history seems to point to "love" as the ultimate solution to humanity's conflicts. The power of love has been preached, taught, and written about for centuries. Perhaps no other single human attribute has received the attention history has given to this subject. Buddha's dissertation on love is a classic, and China has its Golden Rule.

Jesus said it as simply as anyone: "Love your neighbor as yourself." This also implies the importance of loving ourselves. Unfortunately, Christian churches for the most part have instilled a powerful guilt concept in many Christians. They talk about love but too seldom apply it.

During a regression session with a client, after the problem has been identified and analyzed we go through an integration process, during which the problem is generally resolved. The most important question we pose to the client is, "Who do you have to forgive?" The answer is almost always the same: "Myself." This may sound unfair or unreasonable, if the client has been violated or killed in the past. However, people need to forgive themselves not only for crimes they have perpetrated, but also for harboring rage and resentment against others.

During over thirty years of listening to clients' life stories, all of the evidence I have accumulated points to one major idea. All of our experiences are lessons, challenges, or opportunities for learning. What happens to us is never important, only the manner in which we react to the experience. When we react with anger, resentment, jealousy or any other negative emotion, we set a pattern of negative energies in motion. These energies are like boomerangs — they fly right back to the originator of the negative energy.

Pain is the inevitable result. I believe pain of any kind, be it emotional, physical, or mental, is a benevolent signal from our own "higher selves" indicating that it is time to examine our attitudes, our motives, and our thoughts, and make some changes. Referring to the first case in this chapter, although Mrs. Brown considered herself to be a good Christian woman, her beliefs were all cerebral. Underneath that very respectable facade she was harboring rage and resentment toward her dead sisters. So cleverly did she deceive herself in order to be comfortable, that she was not even aware of her anger. However, there is an all-knowing part of us, a "soul-knowledge" if you will, that never lets us off of the hook until we learn the meaning of love and express it.

The only real freedom any of us have is the freedom to choose the way we react to every situation life presents to us. When we react to the vicissitudes in our experience with anger, resentment, fear, guilt or any other negative emotion, we are literally creating blueprints for pain and illness in the future.

Humanity, on a global scale, is just beginning to realize the power of the mind. Our minds are fantastic power centers of creative energy. Almost anything people's minds can conceive, they can achieve. For too long these creative powers have been used without conscious direction, and the consequences in human suffering are everywhere evident. With greater awareness on the part of individuals, and a clearer understanding of the powers of love, compassion, and service, a better world is a distinct possibility.

Mrs. Brown was living a life of self-deception. We all have our dark sides. That is part of being a human being. Life deals with us in response to our hidden agenda. We may think we are loving and caring, unprejudiced, non-judgmental, living up to our own criteria of a good "Christian." However, if the dark side of us is selfish, harbors resentments, carries a heavy burden of guilt (this is, of course, all in the subconscious part of the personality), that is the energy that attracts the multitudinous daily problems so common in the average person's life. However, when insight comes, as it did for Mrs. Brown, the change can be a veritable miracle. Not only did she feel free of that unconscious burden, but she automatically negated any power outside of herself that could harm her.

It should be pointed out that Mrs. Brown's background in metaphysical studies gave her the power to change quickly. Insight came instantaneously because of her understanding of spiritual laws. She had not been aware that she was violating her own belief system. She did not even realize that she still harbored hate. For many who make this discovery, the road to forgiveness and the process of letting go of rage can be slow and painful. At the present time, regression therapy seems to be the quickest and most effective method. It creates a situation in which the individual can examine his/her own role in the drama as he/she created it. In addition, the purpose behind the situation can generally be seen and understood as it relates to the destiny pattern of the individual. From this insight, major changes in the person's emotional patterns are common occurrences.

In the next chapter we will discuss benevolent spirit visitors, and some of the many reasons discarnates occasionally visit the earth plane. These former earth residents may return for the purpose of delivering a last message, or to check periodically on former loved ones. Sometimes they come for the purpose of comforting a grieving friend or relative. Because of the fear which their presence almost always elicits from the visited individual, this can often be a painful encounter.

CHAPTER 6

Periodic Benevolent
Visitors

Spirit visitors often come to our dimension to check on loved ones or to give comfort to their friends or families. The evidence seems to indicate that such entities are spiritually knowledgeable and have the freedom to come and go at will, from one energy level to another. According to metaphysical teachings, the universe consists of levels of awareness, or vibrations. At each point in its spiritual evolution, each individual soul exists on a specific level. Perhaps the most common and best known of these levels is the astral plane, the level just above the physical plane. The so-called earthbound spirits dwell in this area. This is also the realm from which a large percentage of physical paranormal phenomena originate, including table-tipping, ouija board responses, rappings, and similar physical activities commonly attributed to earthbound spirits.

While it is true that malicious spirits reside on the astral plane, not all astral spirits are malevolent. According to esoteric teachings, each major level consists of seven developmental steps. In the astral plane, seven levels measure the spiritual progress of the individual soul. It is said that when one moves from the Astral to the Mind level, an energy form is shed, just as the soul leaves the physical body when one leaves the physical plane. The part that is shed is what we call a ghost. This energy form is without intelligence, and gradually dissolves or disintegrates in the same way that the physical body decays.

Higher levels on the spiritual plane will be discussed in future chapters. For now let us return to the subject of periodic visitors who come to check on their loved ones, or to comfort someone in need.

A Matriarch's Periodic Visits

An old stone house in Riverside, California, has housed the same family for four generations. At the present time three generations dwell there: a mother, her daughter, and the daughter's small child. They have no problems with the spirit manifestations that occur in their house, accepting them as normal activity. None of the manifestations were in any way disruptive to their lives. They believed that their mother-grandmother often visited them in a loving, caring way.

One manifestation troubled them, however, because of what it implied. In the family's past a very young child had died, and her image had been memorialized in a stained glass window at the end of the library. Many visitors asked if there was a baby in the house because they heard one crying. The family also heard the crying periodically. When we visited the house this phenomenon had not manifested for a considerable length of time and we were unable to explain it to the family. Apparently, whatever had held the baby spirit to the house had been dissipated.

When they called and invited us to visit the house, they were curious about the apparent visits of the matriarch. This spirit seemed to appear approximately every three months. Gertrude and I sat on the lovely patio surrounded by exotic plants and enjoyed the gracious hospitality of our two hostesses, mother and daughter, as they served us tea from the elegant family silver.

They related many paranormal incidents that had occurred over the years in the old house. We were able to answer many of their questions about these events. They had numerous stories to share, but very little knowledge about the dynamics of the phenomena. Gertrude made a tour of the house and picked up interesting information psychically, but she was certain no spirits were in the house at the time of our visit. She asked if we might return at another time since she sensed that it would be productive.

A week later we visited the old house a second time. Almost immediately upon entering, Gertrude encountered the spirit of the grandmother, who welcomed her graciously. They conversed, telepathically of course, and she made a special request of Gertrude. She wanted Gertrude to assure the family that she was not earthbound and could go wherever she pleased. She was very busy in her dimension and having a wonderful time. She explained that she still remembered and loved her children and grandchildren and visited them about every three months, earth-time, just to bring them her loving energy and see how they were doing.

She then told Gertrude that there was something in the house of which she was especially fond, and she wanted her daughter to show it to Gertrude and me. She would not tell us what it was, because it was something of a test for all of us and a substantiation of her visit. The daughter and granddaughter immediately thought of an artifact in the room which had been her bedroom, and which had been left unchanged since her death.

We all climbed the stairs and entered the elegantly-appointed, old-fashioned room, truly a museum of fine art, furniture and knickknacks. They approached a particularly lovely figurine and told us that this had been a favorite of their mother and grandmother. But the spirit told Gertrude that was not what she had in mind. So the daughter took us to the dining room and showed us another treasure, this one in the china cabinet. Again the spirit told us that it was not the object she wanted us to see.

Puzzled, the daughter and granddaughter conferred a few moments, then directed us to follow them. They climbed another set of stairs and pointed to an oil painting hanging on an opposite wall. The spirit was delighted and immediately said proudly, "That's it. I painted that."

After a few more words of endearment to her family, delivered through Gertrude, and an expression of her own appreciation for our assistance, she said good-bye and left. Both mother and daughter were grateful for our help and delighted to have a clearer understanding of their ancestor's visits.

A Frightening Encounter

One day the doorbell rang, followed immediately by a loud banging on my front door. I raced to the door to face a distraught young man of my acquaintance. He was almost hysterical as he stammered out his plea for help. He pointed to the car parked in front of my house and told me that his wife was in the car. She had seen her father, who had been dead for two years, and was terrified. He wanted me to go out and talk with her.

I went to the car and got into the seat beside her. She was crying hysterically, her body trembling in fear. Placing my arm around her shoulder I asked her to tell me what had happened. She explained that she had been at home, sitting on the sofa crying. She and her husband had quarreled and she was afraid their marriage was not going to work. All of a sudden she felt a presence and, looking up, saw her father standing a few feet from her. He looked perfectly natural and as real as if he possessed a physical body. He smiled at her and said, "It's all right, dear, don't cry. It is going to be all right." She had screamed in terror and he had instantly disappeared.

She was convinced that she was losing her mind. From her point of view, there could be no other explanation. First I assured her she was not losing her mind, and I explained to her that I knew many people who meditated, attended classes, and tried very hard to have the kind of an experience which she had had naturally. I emphasized the fact that many people experience such encounters, and I described how some people were more sensitive than others. Since she knew me and had confidence in whatever I said, she very quickly became calm and stopped crying.

We talked for about an hour, mostly about her fears regarding her marriage problems. She had many questions also about death and survival. When she let go of her fear, it was comforting to her to believe that her father still cared for her and had come to alleviate her fears.

This experience opened new doors for this young woman and her husband. They both accepted that life was more than a narrow three-dimensional world. However, as far as I know the young lady had no more encounters with a spirit. Many years later I found her to be still interested in psi phenomena, and when a relative died she contacted me to find a medium who might help the son of the dead woman communicate with his mother.

Such contact between the living and the spirits of their loved ones is quite common. It results when a sensitive person experiences emotional conflict of some kind. In all probability such visitations would be even more common if people were not so frightened of them. In all the cases I have known, the visiting spirit withdrew immediately when the person they had visited became frightened. Spirits do not wish to cause harm or distress when they come in response to the suffering of someone they care about. When the one visited shows fear, the spirits immediately withdraw, disappointed that they were not able to give the comfort they are capable of giving.

A Loving Farewell

In contrast to the visitation described above, a similar case occurred in which the client was not afraid. This young woman enrolled in one of my parapsychology classes, and had attended two sessions when her father became very ill and died. One of the major purposes of my classes has always been to acquaint students with the life-death process, and help them accept the cyclical nature of life. Birth on the earth is death in the spiritual dimension, and death on the earth is birth in that other realm. So the idea that life ends with death is a tragic myth to which many people have adhered for centuries. This belief probably causes more anguish than any other, making death the arch enemy and the ultimate tragedy for many people.

When my young friend attended my class for the third session, she approached me and asked to speak with me alone. She was smiling and announced that she wanted to thank me for those first two sessions. She went on to say that they had given her a whole new view of death. After the doctor told her that her father was dying, she sat by her father's bed in the hospital and held his hand. She lovingly told him it was okay for him to go, and that she would be all right. She assured him of her love and thanked him for being such a wonderful father to her.

He died happily, holding her hand.

She went on to tell me that the day after his death she was working in her kitchen and sensed a presence. Turning around she saw her father a few feet from her. Only his torso and head were materialized. It was as if he had no lower body, yet the upper part was as real as a person in the flesh. She started toward him to embrace him, but he smiled and vanished. She had the feeling that he simply wanted to assure her of his after-death reality.

As she stood there describing her experience she told me that prior to attending my class she had been afraid of death and would have been very emotionally upset when her father died. She was quite convinced that somehow she had been prompted to take the class so that she would be better prepared for his departure.

I have found that excessive grieving almost always is a cover for guilt, even though the subject is totally unaware of that fact. Anger and resentment also play a major role, and then the individual feels guilty for his anger. This syndrome, commonly recognized by therapists, is also evident to any observant person. In some cases, one person may feel responsible for the death of another. Their grief appears to be pain brought on by loss, but it is actually the result of their guilt. Children may think they are grieving for a lost parent when the real cause of their tears is rage at the parent for leaving them. All of these hidden causes for grief following death can be alleviated and often totally eliminated when adequate counseling is obtained. Past-life therapy is particularly beneficial in such cases, for it puts the sufferer in direct contact with his/her own hidden agenda.

Some People Need Proof

Freda, one of my very good friends, moved into my neighborhood in the late 1940s with her husband, Frank. She had been an elementary school teacher for many years; Frank was a physical science teacher in a middle school. One morning over coffee we discovered to our mutual delight that we had both been interested in parapsychology for many years, but had never discussed it. In that decade one's intellectual capacities were definitely in question if one took extrasensory perception seriously. From that day on we spent many hours discussing the subject and sharing our individual encounters.

Frank was stubbornly "scientific." In spite of Freda's ESP demonstrations, he refused to believe such things could happen. Whenever she described, in advance, the details of some place they were to visit in their travels, he would insist either that it was a coincidence, or that she must have read the details in a magazine. Once she described their son's clothing as he sat in front of his pup tent while serving in the war. When they received a picture of him in the T-shirt she had described, Frank just laughed and called it a lucky guess on her part. This sort of mild conflict had gone on for years. She was a very loving, non-aggressive individual and refused to try to change her husband or argue with him, but over the years she would quietly interject her experiences, just to share her life with him. He could never bring himself to admit or accept that any of the incidents might be paranormal. It was to his credit, however, that he did not make fun of her.

Freda often thought about finding evidence that she could present to him that would not fit into his scientific model of the world. She was aware that their home housed two or three benevolent spirits, for she could feel their presence. She believed they were there to help and protect her. The two following incidents seemed to provide the answer she had been seeking.

One day she decided she wanted to wash the glasses in the cupboard, which had become cloudy from disuse. At this time she and Frank were both retired, and he often helped her around the house. She washed the glasses, one dozen of them, and he dried. Finishing the washing, she turned to put the glasses back in the cupboard, and found only ten glasses on the counter. She said, "Frank, what did you do with the other two glasses?" He looked surprised and assured her that he had done nothing with them, except wipe each one after she washed it.

They discussed the situation, both denying any knowledge of where the two glasses could have gone. Both were frustrated and incredulous, since neither one of them had left the sink while they were washing and drying the glasses. A look around the kitchen was unproductive. Two drinking glasses had mysteriously disappeared. They finally had to give up the search. The next day both glasses were discovered resting together on the bottom shelf of a china cabinet in the dining room. The cabinet had closed glass doors that fastened tightly when pushed shut.

Frank was visibly shaken by this, for he knew Freda had never left his side and he knew he had not put them there. Freda was delighted. She believed someone was trying to help her give Frank proof that he could not refute.

A second episode occurred a few days later. The two of them were making their king-sized bed, one on each side as they put on the bedding. Frank noticed an object on his side of the bed and said, "What is that on the sheet? Looks like an earring." He picked it up and handed it to Freda. She was amazed and explained to him that it was indeed one of her earrings, which she kept in a locked box inside another, larger box. She had not worn them for years. They were from her mother's collection of jewelry.

They went together to look in the box. She found it in the closet after a few minutes of searching. Laying it on the dresser, she opened the outer box. Then she hunted for the key, which she found in a drawer. When they unlocked the tiny jewel box, there lay the mate to the earring that Frank had found on the bed. Freda, of course, was overjoyed at this manifestation and mentally thanked her spiritual benefactor for providing such incontrovertible evidence for her husband. He, needless to say, was quite speechless, but managed to tell her there had to be a reasonable explanation, even if he could not think of one.

That experience, however, did shake his scientific nature profoundly, and he was willing to talk with her about her rather frequent paranormal experiences. They both went to Hawaii on a vacation and he succeeded in doing a fire-walk in a Huna ceremony, declaring that his feet felt only a little warmth. He was delighted with this experience, but seldom could be induced to talk about it.

It is interesting to speculate on the *modus operandi* for such occurrences. Do they represent spirit intervention for the purpose of providing proof of their ability to intervene in human affairs? Or does a living mind, with its infinite capacity to create, control, and influence energy, find some way to bring about these seemingly impossible paranormal manifestations? The science of electronics may give us some clues, if not the answers, in the near future. At this point we can no longer question the phenomena — these strange things do happen. But how?

A Missing Button

An experience of another friend poses the same type of questions. She and her husband went to the mountains on a picnic in Idyllwild, California. As they were leaving the picnic area, she discovered that one of her sweater buttons was missing. She was very upset and insisted she would not leave until it was found. She had purchased the sweater especially for the buttons and they were expensive. They spent over half an hour hunting through the leaves and pine needles where they had eaten their lunch, but could not find the missing button.

After she arrived home she spent considerable time in the next two days thinking of the button and declaring rather angrily that it was her button and she was not going to give it up. She insisted she wanted it back. On the morning of the third day, as she stood in front of her mirror at her dressing table, she glanced down to pick up a comb. There lay her button.

Such experiences are really not uncommon. Many people have reported such events. Does a friendly spirit transport these objects, or is the mind powerful enough to direct a totally objective force to do its bidding?

Visit to Clarify a Misconception

The following case out of my own experience is being included at length for three reasons. First, I wish to share an unusual relationship between a mother and daughter. It included some very unpleasant encounters, but illustrates spiritual growth on the part of the two people involved. Second, I want to pay tribute to a truly remarkable lady. Finally, I hope to present a background which will provide the reader with enough information to appreciate the sort of very personal connection and understanding that can continue following a death.

When I was growing up I thought I had the best mother in the world. She made certain that I understood the rules, but she was loving and gentle and I wanted to please her. Perhaps the only thing I resented about her was that she was afraid of my father's anger. Although I expected protection from her, she did not protect me from his physical abuse. I learned when I was older that she realized he would be much more violent if she crossed him.

During my teen years she was especially understanding, and I never wanted to do anything I could not share with her. One significant incident comes to mind. I received a letter from a boyfriend, but my father took the letter from the mailbox. He handed it to my mother and told me I could not have it until she had read it. I was furious but obviously helpless. She took the letter and later gave it to me unopened.

My mother and father separated when I was almost sixteen. Mother and I moved from Illinois to California to live with my grandparents. My grandfather, a doctor, had retired in California to be near a number of relatives. Mother soon met a man who loved her very much; seven years later they were married. Mother was a natural scholar. She loved music, art, and lectures and read avidly. My stepfather was a kind, gentle man, but he shared none of Mother's interests, except traveling. His idea of a pleasant evening was playing cards. Because Mother's creative interests were not shared she became a very frustrated wife, loving her husband and feeling stifled at the same time. When he died she had to find employment. For many years she commuted to Los Angeles, where she had an excellent job with Los Angeles County. Everyone who knew Mother loved her,

By the time she retired, with honor and fanfare, she had become considerably set in her ways. I found it exceedingly difficult to let her be whatever she had to be, for I did not want to see her being so rigid and opinionated. On the one hand, she was interested in metaphysics, believed in reincarnation, and resented the fact that I was too busy to spend time with her and talk about my work. On the other hand, she could not demonstrate the beliefs she claimed to accept. She had three locks on her doors, would not open her windows at night, was afraid to travel, resisted going out and making new friends, and demanded more time from me than I had to give. When my husband and I took her for a ride in our car, which we often did on a Sunday, she criticized everything in sight from the color of the houses to the landscaping.

She lived around the corner from me and constantly called me on the phone. She would ask me to come at once, because she needed something "right now." As time went on I became more and more frustrated. This resulted in my feeling angry with her, which was very upsetting to me. I would walk home from her house seething with rage, mostly at myself for letting her upset me so much. As I stomped angrily along, one of the most valuable lessons of my life occurred right in the middle of the sidewalk between our two houses. It was as clear as if someone joined me and walked beside me, speaking rather firmly. "You should thank your mother for staying here long enough for you to overcome this."

It had never been difficult for me to let other members of my family, including my husband, be whatever they had to be. I never tried to run their lives or give them advice unless they asked for it. But my mother? That was a different matter. That short sentence was very pointed — a sharp point that hit the mark. I was not demonstrating one of my own beliefs, that we have no right to coerce or try to control another person. I had been trying to change my mother for a number of years, and it couldn't work. She had to be herself, and experience the consequences of her own behavior.

I can never describe in words the relief I felt, the annoyance with myself for being so blind to what I was doing, and the change that instantly occurred in our relationship. It was as if all resentment and frustration instantly left me. I felt a flood of love for her, and a surge of understanding of her right to experience her own lessons. My friends noticed and commented on the change in me. I felt as if I had graduated to a new level of insight. I have always wanted to be able to demonstrate the beliefs I hold and teach, but I had certainly been blind for a time to the fact that I was out in left field in my attempts to change Mother.

Our relationship improved markedly. I took care of Mother for almost twenty-five years (she died at the age of ninety-two). During this time I had the wonderful experience of sharing her thoughts about what she called "her transition." She looked forward to it and even had me help her pick out the dress and jewelry she wanted to wear. She wrote poetry and selected the poems she wanted read at her service. One day she said, "Isn't it fun to be able to talk about my transition this way? I'll bet not many people can do that."

Now and then she would jokingly promise to get in touch with me from the other side, but after she left I did not feel or experience any contact from her, nor did I try to encourage it. I believed that she would not remain earthbound and needed to be entirely free. One day about three months after she left I was visiting with my psychic friend Freda when she stopped suddenly, looked startled and said, "Your mother has just come in."

Although I could not see her, I was not about to reveal my insensitivity. I also did not want to reject the prospects of communication with Mother, so without hesitating I said, "Well hello, Mother, how are you?" Freda told me that mother was very happy and busy. She wanted me to know that now she understood why I had not had as much time for her as she expected, and she wanted to be sure I knew that she was very proud of me and the work I was doing. She finished by saying she loved me. Then she was gone. I have not been aware of any other visits. I am sure she is now able to express her many talents freely and creatively in her dimension.

During the years I cared for her I know there were times when she was very angry at me for "being too busy to spend more time with her." I believe her brief visit was her way of letting me know she forgave me as well as herself, because she now understood the nature and importance of my work. When we carry anger or misunderstandings with us at death, there is a deep soul need to reconcile that burden. In some cases, such as my mother's, the soul has the opportunity to release that burden without waiting for a new incarnation and the return to another body to work it out. In our case both souls benefited. Her visit relieved her of the guilt she carried because of her anger and misunderstanding of my behavior, and gave me real joy to know that she finally understood why I did not spend more time with her, and that I did love her.

A Father's Last Farewell

A similar type of short visit came soon after my father-in-law died. My husband took care of his father for about seventeen years, before he left at the age of ninety-two. He spent the last few months in a rest home. My husband visited him almost every day on his way home from his office. My husband was not much interested in parapsychology or metaphysics, although he supported me in whatever I wanted to do. Perhaps his lack of contact with sensitives or psychics explains why the following incident happened to me and not to him.

One of my favorite clairvoyants lived near Riverside. As I visited her one day she looked up, surprised, and remarked, "I did not know your father-in-law had passed on. He has just come in." She had never known him, but I confirmed her statement. Hoping I was facing in the right direction, I said, "Hi, Daddy, how are you?" She then described him accurately, including not only his physical appearance but his attitude as well. She said that he did not wish to intrude. He just wanted us to know that during those many weeks at the rest home, even when he did not recognize us he was aware of our visits. He wanted to thank us for being so loving and caring. It had made him very happy to feel our love. Then he was gone. My husband was able to accept my description of his father's visit, and it pleased him.

Brief visits of this kind from discarnates, apparently to bring comfort and reassurance of their well-being, are extremely common. Dozens of people have shared such experiences with me, particularly following a lecture; they decided it was safe to tell me and that I would not laugh at them. I believe such contacts would be even more common if people were not so frightened. Thanks to the escalating interest in paranormal events, that kind of fear is being gradually dispelled.

In the next chapter we will discuss spirits who seem to be bound to the earth by strong, emotional attachments beyond their control. The loved one on the earth plane cannot release the departed spirit. From the evidence available at the present time, it would seem that souls who are held to the earth by powerful energies from grieving friends and relatives suffer continual frustration and pain. They are literally entrapped and cannot move on to the freedom they are entitled to experience when they no longer have a physical body.

CHAPTER 7

Bound by Loved Ones

A Son's Attachment

A long-distance call from a young man who lived in the Victorville, California, area initiated the following case. He said that his house was haunted and explained that his wife had seen the spirit on a number of occasions. His wife's description of what she saw seemed to fit his mother, who had died a few months before. He wanted to believe she was still with him.

The thing that bothered him the most was that, although he loved his mother and was still grieving for her, it was his wife who had seen her. He could not understand why she would show herself to his wife, who barely knew her.

As I talked with this young husband it was obvious that he was totally obsessed with his grief. He was not dealing with his mother's departure realistically. I agreed to meet with him in his home, and Gertrude and I made the trip together. We realized that our real responsibility was going to be to help this young man handle his grief and let his mother go.

When we arrived we met the man and his wife and spent about an hour listening to their report of the events that had occurred in the house. Both he and his wife had heard a series of knockings at night, and the sound of footsteps in the hall. On three occasions his wife had seen a woman at the end of the hall, so clearly that she could describe her features. However, at each manifestation, when the wife screamed the figure disappeared instantly.

We explained that one reason the wife saw the spirit and the husband did not was probably that the wife, although unaware of her ability, was a natural sensitive. The husband did not have this sensitivity; perhaps he did not believe in survival after death in the first place. He corroborated our theory. This was undoubtedly one of the reasons that his mother's death was causing him so much pain. He had loved her very much and could not accept the idea that she no longer existed. He wanted to believe. The noises and his wife's vision had plunged him into a state of conflict between his desire for proof of her survival and his logical conviction that she was gone forever.

During this conversation, Gertrude asked permission to explore the house and left us. She often did this in haunted houses, since it was easier for her to contact presences if she was alone in a room with them. She returned shortly and told us she had a very clear and special message for the son. The mother spirit had explained that she was very unhappy being earthbound but could not get away. Her son thought of her constantly and with so much grief that the energy held her to him. She had tried very hard to prove that she was still a living spirit.

This of course accounted for the manifestations. She had asked Gertrude to tell her son that she wanted him to stop thinking of her all the time, and give that love and attention to his wife instead.

He seemed to accept what we told him. He was very distressed at the thought that he had caused his mother so much discomfort. He seemed to feel that there was enough physical evidence for him to be able to believe in her survival, and he assured us he would work at letting her go. Gertrude reported that the mother was greatly relieved and left before we did.

When I called them two weeks later they assured me that there had been no more manifestations. They felt the problem had been resolved. The wife reported that her husband was much relieved and no longer seemed depressed.

A Mother's Grief

Certainly one of the most traumatic experiences is that of a mother who loses a dearly loved child. In this case the little girl was a second child, nine years old, sensitive and beautiful. She contracted spinal meningitis; the disease paralyzed her digestive tract. She was fed intravenously for three months but slowly wasted away and starved. Her family was devastated and her mother could not control her grief.

On the third night after the funeral the mother was lying in bed, weeping hysterically, when she became aware of a presence standing at the foot of her bed. She lay in quiet amazement as the misty form took shape. There stood her little daughter as real as she had been in the flesh, wearing what had been her favorite dress. Around her were other vague figures, surrounding her in a bright light almost like a halo.

Her daughter spoke in a gentle, loving, but pleading voice. "Mother, please do not grieve for me. I am very happy here. Please let me go." Gradually the vision faded away; except for some light which came through the window from the street lamp, the room was dark. The mother lay very still and felt a profound sense of peace pervade her body like a benediction.

Thoughts began to form in her mind. Uppermost was the question, "Why?" Why had this lovely child with her sweet nature been cut off from life so young? As she traced the little girl's life she became acutely aware of the pain the child had endured. When her daughter was three years old the family moved to an undeveloped wilderness area in Michigan. She recalled how frightened her daughter had been of the animals and of the harshness of their life there. Most of all, she had been frightened of her father. He was a demanding man and insisted on instant obedience from his children. The little girl had suffered harsh physical punishment on numerous occasions. As the mother recalled this and other incidents, she felt a deep sense of sadness and guilt for not having intervened.

Then she thought of her other two children, an older daughter and a younger son, both of whom seemed to be stronger and able to cope with life more successfully than their sister could. For a period of time the mother seemed mesmerized. It was as if she could see the whole scenario. The little girl could not handle the pain in her life. As the mother remembered one particular beating, it occurred to her that that experience might have broken the child's spirit. She had never been quite the same following that event.

These powerful images concluded with a very real feeling that her little daughter had wanted to leave her harsh earth life and be free. This experience considerably reduced the pain of the mother and she made a real effort to be happy for her daughter.

When questioned, the mother could recall no other time in her life when she had manifested any kind of extrasensory ability. Years after this event she reported that it was still very clear. She was certain that her daughter's spirit had communicated an explanation for her departure in order to relieve her mother's pain. Fortunately, this mother did not react to her visitation with fear as so many do, and she was able to receive the insight and comfort her child brought her.

A Father's Self-Entrapment

One of the longest and most interesting cases we investigated involved a radio studio in San Bernardino, California. The initial call came from Raymond, an employee in the station. He was afraid to talk about his experiences for fear of ridicule from his fellow employees. When he was alone, working on cassettes, he would hear loud sounds coming from another room. Sometimes it would be a banging noise, other times a crunching sound like heavy boots walking on loose gravel. The sounds occurred nightly, sometimes a number of times in one evening.

Eventually one of the other men, who occasionally worked on Raymond's nights off, asked him if he had heard strange noises in the studio. This opened the door to a discussion. They compared notes, agreeing on the unaccounted-for sounds. Raymond invited a friend who was a spiritualist minister to investigate. Her two visits failed to reveal any information. When she was there nothing unusual occurred. She could only report that she felt some sort of energy which was not malevolent. Beyond that she could not identify it or get any message from it.

Then one day, in the presence of the entire office staff, a cassette left the shelf, floated slowly through the air, and landed gently on the floor. It soared right past the desk of the manager, who threw up his hands and yelled, "What the hell is going on here?" Needless to say, the office was a turmoil of speculation. Everyone swore everyone else to silence, most of them thoroughly convinced that someone in the office was playing a prank of some kind.

Raymond heard about us through a friend and called me for help. Gertrude and I were delighted by the sound of this case, for it seemed to promise some unusual aspects of the haunting phenomenon. When we walked through the door of the studio, Gertrude immediately began to converse with the spirit. She could carry on a telepathic communication, of course, but for my benefit she always verbalized her side of the conversation.

The spirit's first question was, "How come you know I am here and can talk to me and no one else can?" She explained her psychic ability; he was delighted. An animated conversation ensued between them, while Raymond and I listened. The spirit's name was Harvey. He explained that his son had been reported missing during the war. He had to stay in this place because he was sure that someday his son would return.

At this point Raymond told us that the studio had once been a duplex. While we were talking, a sudden loud crunching sound seemed to come from the next room. Raymond identified it as the sound he often heard. I had brought my tape recorder as usual. I asked Harvey if he would repeat the sound for my recorder. He obligingly complied. I asked him three more times just to be sure it was no coincidence and he repeated the sound for me each time.

We asked Harvey why he moved tapes around and scared people. He said, "Do you realize how boring it is just sitting around here all the time waiting for my son?" He told us he had experimented to see what he could do to get the attention of people in the studio. This helped to pass the time so he did not get so bored. When he succeeded in manifesting physically it was really funny to watch people's reactions.

Finally it was time to introduce the idea that he could be free and did not have to stay in the studio to find his son. We explained that if he would ask for help and open his mind to the dimension he now occupied he would find a new freedom. He could go anywhere he wanted, perhaps even find his son. He was skeptical and asked why someone had not told him this before. It is not always easy to explain that the beliefs held in the mind manifest as reality to the believer. Since he believed that this physical world is all there is, he could deal only with that reality. He could not countenance his own death, and therefore could not open his mind to explore other possibilities.

However, we were able to provide evidence that he could accept regarding his own condition. When it was pointed out to him, he had to agree. He decided he would investigate our claims and proceed from there. He thanked us profusely and for our interest in him, and for being so patient.

We never heard any more of Harvey. When we checked with Raymond a week or so later, he reported that there had been no further evidence of Harvey's presence. The studio was peaceful and back to normal. As far as we know, Raymond never did tell the studio staff why there were no more strange happenings. He had told us he had no intention of trying to explain the experience we shared with him, when Gertrude drew the curtain on the other dimension and we spent an evening in lively conversation with a spirit.

A Sister's Fears Explained

The following case is included for its unique combination of paranormal aspects. It explains a phobia, demonstrates the power of fear and guilt to hold two people in bondage, shows the value of involving a psychic, and provides an example of the successful employment of table-tipping. In addition, it introduces a series of events that seem to be orchestrated by an intelligence beyond the conscious power of the individuals involved.

Through the years I have taught many classes and study groups interested in parapsychology and metaphysics. One such group involved nine high school girls who came to my home after school once a week. They were particularly interested in hypnosis and brought written notes from their mothers giving me permission to hypnotize them. However, one of them could not relax and respond to the induction, even though she said she wanted to and was trying to cooperate. After three meetings of the group she was still unsuccessful. This caused her to feel inadequate and embarrassed, in spite of my assurance that it was all right and not that important. I explained that many people block hypnosis, for reasons which are not always known.

On the very first meeting of the group, I recognized that one of the girls had exceptionally high clairvoyant ability. She had not been aware of this and was delighted, but also a little afraid. However, she was a very serious girl with high integrity. She determined to utilize her ability for useful purposes.

One day these two girls arrived for the meeting, but no one else came. We waited a few minutes. The two girls reported that they had seen all of the others at lunch and their parting words had been "We'll see you later at the meeting."

Deciding we would wait no longer, I asked if they wanted to discuss the planned subject or something else. They both responded that they wanted to tip tables. We had never done this in the group. I always discourage it, pointing out the potential dangers of inviting undesirable discarnates to come in and communicate, unless the experience is controlled by a psychic who is knowledgeable and can protect the sitters.

Their request seemed so urgent that my intuitive response was positive. I brought out a TV tray. I sat on one side and Julia, the young lady who was afraid of hypnosis, sat opposite me. The psychic Marjorie sat at the end of the table. The moment our fingers touched the surface of the tray it began to rock violently back and forth. I was frankly astounded, for I had never seen a table respond so rapidly and with such vigor.

Julia looked across the table at me with wide-eyed surprise. In a startled voice, she said, "Mrs. Denning, my brother is here." Her brother had died two years before, a fact which I had not been aware of prior to this moment. In a matter-of-fact voice Marjorie stated, "Of course he is here. That is the reason for this meeting." Then she explained that the brother was very distressed because Julia believed that she had been responsible for his death. He had not been able to move on in his world because of her constant guilty feelings reaching him. He explained that his death was his own responsibility and right for his own evolving destiny. He assured Julia that she had nothing to do with it. Marjorie reported that he blessed his sister and, after saying good-bye, he departed.

The TV tray had stopped moving following Julia's first startled remark. She later could not explain how she knew it was her brother. She said, "I just KNEW!" As the three of us discussed what had happened, Julia described her feelings as having a heavy weight lifted from her chest and heart.

All of us were deeply impressed with the fact that the other girls had not come that day. We speculated on who or what kept them from coming. All of us were quite certain that something had planned this encounter and kept them away. Needless to say, all three of us sensed that a benevolent power had operated through us on behalf of Julia.

At the next meeting of the group Julia had no trouble being hypnotized. Her fear had been caused by her guilt. She had been afraid that what she might see would convict her of causing her brother's death.

The dynamics of this case are quite provocative. First we have Julia's phobia, her fear of hypnosis. Whenever people block hypnosis, it is important to look for the cause. This is usually found in some kind of fear, although in some cases the person wants to succeed so desperately that tension prevents success. However, this too is fear: fear that he/she can't go into a trance.

This case provides an excellent example of how fear and guilt can lock two people from different dimensions in bondage until spiritual insight and a higher understanding liberates them. In this case, did the brother instigate the events that led to the liberation of himself and his sister? Did Julia's higher self create the scenario? Or did the events result from cooperation on the part of the spirit guides of both? It must have taken some special ingenuity to keep all of the other girls from attending that meeting. Who was responsible for that bit of maneuvering? We do not know the answers to these questions. There may be truth in all of the suggested possibilities.

Let us not overlook the importance of the psychic in this drama. As a general rule, I advise people to be their own psychics, to find their answers within their own all-knowing minds. Sometimes, however, an individual with this gift, who has integrity and a desire to help others, can be of tremendous help when the people involved are blocked.

Now add the TV tray. Although a gimmicky phenomenon, we have seen success of a high order result from the use of such tools. This is an excellent example of the importance of evaluating each case individually, for I have also known more harm than good to come from the use of physical paraphernalia. The criteria for positive results seems to be the motive and spiritual development of the operators.

To summarize briefly, it appears that we know very little about the actual dynamics of much of the phenomena we observe. It behooves us at this time to continue our search for the cause of the many remarkable and seemingly miraculous manifestations of the magnificent universe we inhabit.

The next chapter addresses a very practical subject. When an individual dies and leaves unfinished business or particular fears, the soul may remain long enough to resolve the problem or the conflict, often helping and guiding the loved one to a resolution.

CHAPTER 8

Practical Assistance for the Bereaved

A Husband's Support

James and Ethel had been married for many years. They enjoyed an exceptionally good relationship, one that had weathered well. They respected each other, loved each other, and were good friends. She had been interested in metaphysics most of her life and was a successful practitioner in the Church of Religious Science. James supported her, but had no personal interest in parapsychology, or in the metaphysical teachings that were so much a part of her life. A successful broker, he was totally absorbed in his own business and his associates. However, James and Ethel shared quality time together. They enjoyed traveling and, as prominent members of the community, attending evening social functions.

I first met Ethel when I was referred to her for help with my two teen-age boys. She was a wise counselor and quickly helped solve my problem. We felt a strong bond from our first meeting, and both believed that the boys were just a means of bringing us together. Ethel was a sensitive and soon picked up the frustrations in my life. She informed me that I should be doing what she was doing, and encouraged me to get myself in gear and go back to school.

73

In one of those dramatic moments in life when one feels the inspiration of truth flooding the very cells of one's body with indescribable energy, I knew the time had come. I had always felt that someday I would return to school. For years I had frequent nightmares in which I could not find my classroom, or came to the end of a semester and realized, to my great distress, that I had overlooked a class I needed, or arrived in class without my homework.

The day after my interview with Ethel I drove to the local junior college and registered for the next semester, which was to begin in approximately six weeks. Suddenly it was as if I was born again. I felt as if I was back on track, and I never had another frustration dream about school.

Ethel and I remained close friends. A few years later I was teaching classes in parapsychology. She was a member of my class; for a time we met in her home. It was at this time that James joined the class. Ethel was delighted. She told me that she did not know what had changed him so much but that every book she brought home to read disappeared from her table, to be returned only after he had read it.

One of the members of this particular class was exceptionally gifted psychically. At a number of the meetings she went into an altered state and answered questions. One evening we asked her to interpret dreams presented by the class members. James described himself standing in front of a large forest which was burning with magnificent brilliance. He did not feel any sadness. Instead, his feelings were of elation and ecstasy over the rare beauty of the scene. Upon awakening he experienced a sensation of awe.

The interpretation given by the psychic was that he was on the verge of a major change in his life, which would be good. Following the meeting the psychic told me the dream was precognitive; it warned of his impending death. She was right. A few days later as he and Ethel were driving he had a heart attack at the wheel of his car. He died instantly, slumped over the steering wheel. At first Ethel was devastated and in shock, but her beliefs about life after death and her metaphysical studies stood her in good stead. She quickly recovered her balance, except that she was afraid to drive.

At the next meeting of the group the psychic informed us that James was present, and very much interested in what we were doing. He told her to tell us that he wanted to thank his wife for getting him interested in metaphysics. His avid reading in that field had made his transition an easy, wonderful experience. He asked if we would be interested in having him describe his transition, his own experience of dying. He suggested we bring a tape recorder to the next meeting and he would tell us how it felt to die. This we did, of course, and he took us step by step through his death experience. He said it was like being catapulted into a brilliant light, too beautiful to describe in words, accompanied by a wonderful euphoria of well-being and joy.

James told us that he had the freedom to go and come as he pleased for what would be about three months in earth time. He was exploring his dimension, visiting friends and loved ones in the physical dimension, and having a wonderful time. He said that eventually he would choose some kind of work in his non-physical world, but he would let us know before he left.

One morning shortly after his death, Ethel walked out onto her front porch with her sister-in-law, who had come to stay with her until she was ready to be alone. There before them on the top step lay a beautiful yellow rose still damp from the morning dew. She picked it up with a rush of emotion, for she had a feeling it was connected with James, although she did not know how.

The psychic and I were meeting weekly to do some research together. At our next meeting I asked her to contact James and inquire about the yellow rose. He was delighted to know we connected it with him. When I asked how he managed it, he explained that he had impressed a child going to school to pick it and then drop it on the porch. Since no yellow roses grew in Ethel's immediate neighborhood, this seemed like a plausible explanation. I had thought it might be an apport, or that he had manifested it. He then told us that he would continue to use a yellow rose as a sign of his love and concern for Ethel.

Shortly after that a psychic who knew nothing of the history of Ethel and James came to our meeting. In her brief message to Ethel she said, "I don't know what it means, but I see a lovely bouquet of yellow roses by your head." Through the weeks that followed, other psychics also saw yellow roses by Ethel.

One evening James gave Ethel a scolding for not driving her car. He said, "I want you to get in that car and drive. I promise I will be right behind you, protecting you from any harm. You must stop being afraid. There is nothing to be afraid of." The psychic reported this message and added that James was very adamant about it. He wanted to make sure that Ethel heeded him, for it was important for her to be independent. He explained that she was beginning to live for our monthly class meetings and that was not healthy for her. He said he would not be around much longer and wanted her to be free before he left.

Then a dramatic incident occurred which was the most powerful evidence we had of his presence. One day a personal friend, who had no knowledge of our meetings, called me. She asked if I knew of a book about Joseph of Arimathea. I told her I did not, but that I was going to a meeting where I would see a man who had visited England and Glastonbury. He was extremely interested in Joseph's history and had gone to England to find his burial place. If anyone knew of such a book, he would.

When I got to the meeting I had forgotten all about the book, and the gentleman I had in mind was absent that night. Shortly after the meeting started the psychic said, "That's strange. James is in his old office looking through the bookshelves."

I told her to ask him if there was anything we could do to help him. She told me he said to go on with our meeting; he did not need anything.

A few minutes later the psychic again said, "How odd. James is now in the dining room, looking through the bookshelves there." Again I suggested she ask if we could help. At that point she said with aroused interest, "He has just selected a book and is holding it up in the air. It is green with gold letters." Of course none of the rest of us saw anything in the air, but I told her to go over and see if she could identify the book.

She walked to the bookshelves and, dropping to her knees, selected a book and held it up. It was white with blue letters. We all felt a wave of disappointment, until she began fumbling with the jacket. She removed it to reveal a green book with gold letters. The gold letters read, "Joseph of Arimathea."

No one in the room knew the significance of this until I explained about the telephone call from my friend. Then the psychic conveyed the message from James. He was laughing. "That's my contribution to the meeting tonight."

On another occasion a visiting psychic joined us. He came at my invitation and did not know any of the members of the group. As soon as he sat down he leaned over to me and asked, "Who is that man sitting in that chair over by the door?" I suggested that he describe the spirit he was seeing. He proceeded to do so, accurately, from James' white hair and partially bald head to his small feet. Later in the meeting when all of us were laughing over something humorous he said, "Well, that is a new one on me. That spirit just took off his glasses and is wiping them and his eyes." Everyone in the room laughed, for we recognized that gesture as being typical of James. He had a delightful sense of humor. Whenever he laughed heartily he always removed his glasses and wiped them and his eyes before putting the glasses back on.

About three months after his death, an evening came when James announced that he would not see us again. He explained that his "vacation" was over. Now he would choose some activity in his dimension. He felt he had supported Ethel through the most difficult time of her adjustment, and to stay any longer would keep her dependent on him. He thanked us for the wonderful experience he had shared with us, and with a few words of love and encouragement to Ethel his energy was gone.

This was an unusually detailed experience played out over a period of time, but it illustrates a loved one's concern and ability to help when there is sensitivity to communication. This account of the saga delineates only some of the highlights of our interchange with this departed spirit. There were many delightful personal exchanges at the meetings. It also makes very clear the value of letting go of loved ones. In this case, because of his own studies and understanding and the advantage he had of seeing from an unobstructed perspective, James was strong enough to resist Ethel's need to hold him. His insight put him in a stronger position, and enabled him to make the decision to terminate their contact. He did, however, have Ethel's cooperation, based on her own understanding of his need to move on.

Unfortunately, although many people have the potential for this kind of support following the loss of a loved one, our western belief system denies the possibility of such contact and so millions of individuals are robbed of the solace it could bring. Much of the pain we feel comes from uncertainty. We are not sure where our loved ones are, or whether they really are still alive in some other place. Even though there is no doubt in my own mind about the continuance of life, it was a great source of comfort to me when my husband contacted me an hour after his heart attack on the tennis court. He said, very clearly, "Honey, I did it, I did it just the way I wanted to." Since tennis was his favorite recreation it was a perfect way for him to go. He had always said he did not want to die in bed with tubes in his nose. That contact was a joyous experience for me because it was so real. I felt his happiness at being free.

I would like to introduce another factor in the death experience. Although it has nothing to do with the major theme of this book, it does have specific significance for the departed loved one. Many people find it impossible to control their grief, which can linger for years. One of the primary reasons for this is guilt on the part of the survivor. In my practice I have encountered this phenomenon many times. Once we deal with the guilt, the grieving stops. Let me make it quite clear that missing a loved one is not the same thing as prolonged grief. Guilt may stem from a number of sources. One common reason is that the survivor feels somehow responsible for the death. "If I had just done this or that," or "If I had not let her go out alone," or whatever speculation fits the specific case, "this would not have happened."

Let me suggest that we are each responsible for ourselves. Even a small child has a destiny over which a parent has no control. Think for a moment: if a psychic can predict events months, even years, in advance, then the event must be in the blueprint of that individual's destiny. There is no longer any doubt that events CAN be predicted in advance. We each have our own role to play on the stage of life, in the great drama in which we all are cast. Although we play into one another's destiny patterns, we are not responsible for another's death. We may very well play a role in it, but as individuals we do not have that much power over another's life.

There are many other reasons for guilt; resenting or hating the person who has gone are both common. Feeling sorry for oneself and nurturing the "poor me" syndrome often brings some solace. Whatever the origin of the guilt, if it is held and nourished in grief it is very painful to the spirit, and makes it difficult for the loved one to move on in the other dimension. Once this pathological connection is truly understood, much of the suffering that presently occurs following death will be markedly reduced.

Employing an Intermediary

One day a client said to me, "My husband has a strange psychic experience to tell someone. He would like to share it with you. He has told no one up to now, although it happened when he was fourteen years old. At the time of the incident he suffered ridicule and rejection by his peers, and reprimands from his parents. He has not wanted anyone to know that he was 'different.' However, he has become interested in sharing it with you because of the things I have told him about you. He feels that perhaps you are someone who would really understand." A few days later the three of us met to have lunch and he told the following story.

When he was fourteen he lived in a small rural town and worked in a mortuary. He ran errands, swept floors, and did odd jobs for the mortician. One day a car accident took the lives of an entire family of seven, and within hours a man died of a heart attack in a local hotel room.

The mortuary was not staffed to handle so many people at once. The mortician instructed the boy to put the body of the man in the refrigerator.

As he wheeled the body into the room he could not resist the temptation to look at the man. So, with a curiosity he could not control, he lifted the cover and stared at the dead face. He had never seen a dead person before. This direct contact made him feel very uncomfortable.

That night when he was in his room preparing for bed a figure materialized before him. It was the man he had seen in the mortuary. His appearance was so terrifying the boy could not move. The spirit uttered words of reassurance, and begged the boy not to be afraid, but to listen. The specter proceeded to explain that his identification had been stolen with his wallet. He was very distressed that his family would not know what had happened to him. He explained that he was a traveling salesman and lived in another state. He gave the boy his family name and address and begged him to notify his relatives of his whereabouts. As the spirit explained his distressing situation the boy's fears diminished, and he agreed to try and contact the man's family.

After the visitor disappeared the boy tried to sleep but found it impossible. The thought of telling his parents about his experience sent shivers of fear up his spine. They would certainly accuse him of lying, or pronounce him crazy. In the morning he finally decided he had to tell them. After all, he had evidence, the address and name, unless they proved to be false information. If they were false, where would he be? In the end he told his mother, she called his father, and after much discussion they decided to tell the mortician.

The mortician was skeptical to say the least but, having nothing else to go on, he took the name and address and was successful in locating the man's family. All would have been well if it had ended there, but such a story was much too unusual to remain a secret. The word got out, and for months the family was persecuted.

Children shunned the boy or made fun of him at school Towns-people avoided the family or threw rocks at their house and paint-ed obscenities on their fence.

News of the incident finally reached the PSI researchers at Duke University. A representative was sent to interview the fami-ly. By that time they were not about to expose themselves to fur-ther harassment. They refused to talk with him. The incident was eventually forgotten and the boy's life returned to normal — or as normal as life can be when one feels "different." At that time there was little information available about such experiences. While this man had no further psychic experiences of any kind that he could recall, he grew up with the belief that he was somehow odd, and that if people knew about his unusual experience they would not accept him.

When his wife became interested in parapsychology and first tried to share her interest with him, he was cautious. Gradually, however, he felt a sense of relief to discover that many people have such experiences. He finally told his wife his story. Much to his relief, she was delighted. By the time he shared his experience with me he had become quite comfortable with talking about it.

Such single encounters with a specific purpose are not at all uncommon. They can occur when the spirit is troubled about something and needs the help of a mortal individual. I believe it is the intensity of the spirit's own emotion that generates enough energy to attract the attention of a living person. All of us have some psychic sense. If we did not, we would be quite unable to function effectively in the physical world. There seems to be evi-dence that spirits can "see" the auric body of a person. The quali-ty or intensity of that auric energy tells the spirit whether or not a certain individual can be impressed with a message. I believe many hunches are the result of this gentle kind of help or guidance from concerned spirits.

Legal Help from the Grave

Numerous stories have come to my attention regarding husbands who return to assist their wives with the legal and financial prob-lems that frequently follow the death of a family provider. One case that I encountered in my own investigations involved a very gentle lady who knew absolutely nothing about business. She was the epitome of the helpless female. Her husband treated her as his most cherished possession. He provided her with a housekeeper who ran the house and was an excellent cook.

The woman had many friends and enjoyed a busy social life, with practically no real responsibilities. They had no children to occupy her time. When her husband died of a heart attack she was totally unprepared to take responsibility for her own affairs.

Shortly after the funeral, feeling abandoned, she was lying in her bed, weeping, when she felt a presence in the room. At first she was frightened, since she knew the housekeeper was out marketing. Then she saw her husband, standing at the side of her bed. He looked at her sadly and assured her that she had nothing to fear. He had come to help her.

She was certain that her mind had snapped, and wondered if she was really going crazy, but his presence carried with it a powerful energy of love and support. Her panic subsided as she listened to him. He explained, in a practical way, where she would find his will, which lawyer to call, and where he kept the key to their safe deposit box. He went on to explain that because his business had suffered some reverses in recent months, she would have to give up their large home and live in smaller quarters. He was very sorry, but her income would no longer support a maid and she would have to learn to cook for herself. He promised to stay with her until everything was settled and she was knowledgeable about her affairs and could manage alone.

She discovered resources within herself which she had never known she possessed. To her surprise she found it challenging and satisfying to do something that had significance. She faced her situation courageously and, salvaging what she could from her husband's business, invested enough to give herself a small, regular income. She had absolutely no marketable skills, for she had never worked for a salary. She sold her home and rented a very small house, which she furnished with her most cherished possessions. Afterwards she sold the rest of their household furnishings.

For a number of weeks, whenever new decisions had to be made she would sit down and ask her husband for help, and he would generally appear. At other times she felt his presence. With her eyes closed she could hear his voice, as though he spoke to her mind. Then one day he told her she no longer needed his help. She was doing well and knew everything about their business that she needed to know to handle her life alone. He reassured her of his love and said good-bye. She felt his energy leave her.

For a moment the room felt very empty and she experienced fear, but the panic reaction left when she told herself she was all right and could take care of herself.

She came to my church, which was close to her new house. She did not drive so she had no car. When I met her she was busily involved in making new friends and creating meaningful activity to occupy her time. She told me that most of the people she had considered her friends were no longer interested in her now that she was "poor." Then she laughed and said, "But I am the richer, for I have now found people who really care and are genuine friends. Losing my money was the best thing that ever happened to me, for I found something my money could not buy. The people in this church opened their hearts to me when I came with my pain. They have given my life new meaning. I have never been so happy."

As long as I was active in that church she was very much involved in its programs. She had many friends. I never saw her when she was not smiling; she expressed a contagious enthusiasm for whatever she was doing. In cases such as this where the spirit returns and makes a specific contact with the loved one, the grieving period is often considerably reduced.

The subject of the next chapter is violent death, and the problems created for the spirits of those traumatic experiences. The fact that many spirits do not know they are physically dead is difficult for most people to comprehend. However, there is a vast amount of evidence that such is the case. Since mind is the only reality we have, reality for each of us is what we perceive. Disembodied entities can see, think, feel, suffer, hear, and experience an awareness of their own reality. Therefore, logically, they assume they are alive. Since many people die with no belief in survival of any kind, in their minds it is not logical that they could be alive without a body.

Four case histories will serve to illustrate the types of problems sudden or violent deaths can create. A growing understanding of this phenomena has opened the way for providing help to these tortured souls. An increasing number of therapists and counselors are skilled in dealing with this little-understood field of therapy.

I would like to point out, however, that this is not a new field, or a significant new discovery in the annals of survival or therapeutic methods. In 1924 a psychiatrist, Dr. Carl A. Wickland, wrote a book entitled *Thirty Years Among the Dead*. It was reprinted once in a condensed version, then reprinted in its entirety in paperback in 1963. The entire volume deals with the work he and his clairvoyant wife contributed to this controversial subject. For thirty years part of their work consisted of liberating entities trapped in the energy field of the earth.

CHAPTER 9

Violent Deaths Create Restless Spirits

Terror at Midnight

Dr. Lewis and I met at a dinner party arranged to bring us together. From our first exchange of pleasantries we were on the same wavelength; for the remainder of the evening we were practically unaware of anyone else. He was an elderly physician with a wealth of knowledge about life and the paranormal field. He was psychic, although he did not claim that ability. It was an absolute joy to converse with him, and we spent the evening exchanging experiences and philosophies.

From him I learned firsthand about phantom limbs. One hears about people who still feel their arms or hands after they have been amputated. The explanation given is that these sensations are products of their imagination. Dr. Lewis told me about a case in his hospital. Hours after a man had his leg amputated he began to complain that his leg was burning. Since he had no leg, the nurse tried to put his mind at ease with the usual reassurances. The man was apparently in so much pain that she called Dr. Lewis to talk with him. Dr. Lewis sent an orderly to find out what had happened to the leg. It had been tossed aside, and was found lying against a very hot radiator, the flesh scorched. After the leg was disposed of properly the man experienced no more burning pain.

This incident happened many years ago, before "energy" had been recognized as the source of all things animate and inanimate. As unscientific as it may sound, the good doctor explained to me that after any amputation the energy or life-force of that lost body part remains with the body. This energy must be drawn up or back into the the body in order for the individual to be comfortable. This can be easily accomplished. The mind visualizes the process, ordering it to take place. The person in charge of the procedure will often use hand passes from the extreme area of the limb up to the body. Explanations of the efficacy of this practice are numerous. Who knows the true explanation of this procedure? The fact remains that it works. Many cases of phantom limb pain have been cured by this simple ritual.

When Dr. Lewis learned that I was interested in haunted houses, he offered to share his most frightening experience with me. One of his friends owned a house that was very definitely haunted. Everyone who slept in a certain room was awakened at midnight by a terrifying apparition in the form of a large, angry-looking man. This specter stood over the bed and held his hands in a threatening manner over the occupant's face. The man's friends and family began to question whether the experience was triggered by fear and expectation, prompted by the rampant stories regarding that room. In other words, did fear create the experience? Was it purely subjective?

They decided to test their theory. A three-year-old child who knew nothing about the apparent hauntings was put to sleep in the room. Promptly at midnight the child screamed in terror, and everyone came running. They found her sitting on the bed, shaking and crying. "A terrible man tried to get me," she stammered between sobs.

When Dr. Lewis heard the story he volunteered to be the next one to sleep in the bed. He declared that he was not afraid of man, beast, or ghosts — and so became the next victim. He awoke from a sound sleep with the hair standing up on his head and the feeling that he was not alone. Opening his eyes, he watched a large man approach his bed and stand over him, huge hands held over his face in a threatening manner. In a firm voice and with as much bravado as he could manage, Dr. Lewis said, "What do you mean scaring everyone? What the hell do you want? If there is something I can do for you, just say so."

The spirit answered apologetically. He explained that he had been murdered in this house, and his body buried in the basement.

He believed his soul could not rest until he had been given a proper Christian interment. He described the exact spot in which his body had been buried and begged Dr. Lewis to help him find peace of mind.

The family that now owned the house agreed to help. Excavations in their cellar unearthed the bones of a grown man, in the exact location the spirit had described. Everyone cooperated in giving him a Christian burial. From that time on, no one who slept in that room was disturbed.

An Unseen Hand of Death

A young Scandinavian couple lived on a small ranch outside of Riverside. One day the wife complained to a neighbor that she was afraid to be in her house alone because of the horrible green thing at the end of her hall. She knew there was really nothing there, but when she tried to walk through it she felt a marked change in temperature; the area was very cold. Her friend told her about me and she called me for help.

Gertrude and I went out to the ranch. The charming young Swedish girl was quite embarrassed about her problem. She was convinced that there was something wrong with her, since her husband seemed to be unaware of anything strange in the house. Gertrude walked through the house and found a very angry spirit hovering at the end of the hall. He was not a very nice fellow. He seemed upset that she had discovered him, and declared that he was not going to leave.

Using her gentle powers of persuasion, as well as some irrefutable logic, Gertrude succeeded in overcoming his fears and resistance. He finally told her his story. He had been in a bar, drinking with his friends, when a violent fight broke out. Within moments, everyone in the room was involved in the fight. Suddenly he found himself out of his body. He looked down and saw himself lying on the floor, blood flowing out of the back of his head. Someone had struck him from the rear with a hatchet, splitting his head wide open. He did not know who had attacked him. His death was so sudden that he was left totally bewildered, and very angry.

He had wandered around for a long time, he thought, until finally he saw a young Swedish man whose aura attracted him. He had been living in Sweden when he was killed, and he felt safer after he found another Swede. He had not meant to frighten the man's wife, but she seemed to know he was there. She always reacted to him with fright, which made him uncomfortable. Although she had not known she was psychic she obviously was, and so his presence affected her.

The spirit had no intention of leaving. The only time he had felt any kind of security was when he was near the young man who, it turned out, had a considerable amount of anger himself. We spent approximately twenty minutes talking with this spirit, explaining that he need no longer be trapped in this way. We told him that there was a whole dimension out there in which he could find some peace of mind. He finally agreed to go with a spirit who came at his request. The young husband admitted that he had been vaguely aware of something strange going on in his house, but he had been afraid of ridicule if he acknowledged this.

At the last follow-up no further manifestations of a foreign presence in the house had occurred. The green blob was gone. The wife had described it as an ugly greenish mist accompanied by an unpleasant odor. This is the only case in our records in which this physical evidence was reported. I do not know the explanation for the color, but odors are not uncommon. One of my friends reported that whenever her father wanted to make his presence known she would smell his cigar smoke. Others have also told me of olfactory communications.

An Accident Creates Trauma

A client recently brought me another case with a similar cause but quite different manifestations. When she called me on the phone she said she was in a terrible state of confusion and could not seem to get her thoughts clear.

We met at my office. She explained that for the past few months, since moving into a new home, she had not been able to unpack some of the boxes, which were still in the garage and on the floor in the house. She "felt" as if something else was in the house. Although she saw nothing, she did hear a few strange noises. She could not identify the sounds or trace them to any human or physical source. She had not told her husband about her feelings. She had nothing concrete to describe, and did not want him to think there was anything wrong with her mind.

Her real concern was her mental confusion. She was a college graduate, a teacher, and an intelligent person. She had always considered herself to be in control of her life. Now she felt as if her head were stuffed with fragments of unfinished thoughts. She found it almost impossible to hold on to an idea and carry it through to completion. As a result she could not accomplish anything, even household tasks such as unpacking the boxes from her move. She could not control the wild thoughts racing through her mind. At times it felt as if she were literally flying apart.

I suspected that in addition to a spirit occupying her house, a discarnate entity had invaded her. With some hesitation, I suggested that she might be possessed. She responded at once with a sigh of relief. She admitted that she had thought this might be the problem but had been hesitant to suggest it.

She was an excellent hypnotic subject. In a matter of seconds I guided her into a deep, altered state of consciousness. I asked if there was anyone in her or with her who would speak to me. Immediately she spoke in a voice not her own. "Oh yes, yes, help me, please help me! I don't know where I am or what happened to me. I am so frightened and I can't find anyone to help me. No one will listen to me."

I directed the speaker to go back to a time before he became so frightened and tell me what had happened to him. He reported that he was walking along a dark street, alone. Then something hit him from behind. That was the last thing he remembered clearly. From that moment on he remembered nothing but confusion. He did not know where he was. He could not figure out what was going on. Finally he saw this nice lady. She seemed to be a kind person. He thought she might be able to help him, but she hadn't. She did not answer him when he tried to talk with her, any more than anyone else had.

It is interesting to note here that while it was true that the woman was a kind, loving person, personal problems involving certain members of her family had kept her in a state of emotional confusion for some months. A combination of her nurturing self and her confused emotional state had attracted this young male spirit. Although she had been coping with her emotional state fairly well on her own, without any mental confusion, she was vulnerable. When the spirit, in his mental turmoil, actually invaded her energy field, she took on his feelings.

I conversed with this confused spirit for about half an hour, explaining to him what had happened and what he could do about it now. He was responsive and receptive, but very hesitant. He did not feel he could walk into the light. He was not good enough. I continued to encourage him to open his eyes and look at the light, explaining that anyone can do that. Finally I used guided imagery to describe a path with flowers on both sides and a light at its end. Finally he was able to open his eyes. He told me the path was beautiful. If it was all right with me, he thought he could walk into it.

Then followed one of the more touching experiences that I have ever had with a spirit. He finally told me he was ready to go into the light and said, "Thank you, oh thank you so much, both of you. Here, I would like to give you a flower to show my thanks." With this statement, my client's arm rose from the arm of the reclining chair. She extended her hand towards me as if she was giving me something. I reached out and "took" whatever it was and said, "Thank you." The spirit responded immediately, "Thank you, and thank you both again for helping me. Goodbye."

My client, still in an altered state, said, "Oh my, what a relief. I feel so good. I am so happy for him. He was so relieved." She came out of her trance state and we talked about her feelings. She said she felt absolutely wonderful and could not find the words to describe the difference in her mind. She felt as if all the fragmented pieces had come together again; she could think clearly. A follow-up a year later confirmed the success of her experience.

Murdered Woman Seeks Help

One day when I answered the phone, a distraught voice on the other end pleaded, "Don't hang up on me, please don't hang up when you hear what I have to tell you." I promised that I would listen to whatever she wanted to tell me. After all, this was not the first time I had heard that request. People having paranormal experiences are often treated like pariahs, and when they call for help are obliged to cope with cruel rejection.

She explained that something in her house was violently harassing her family. She had been jerked out of her bed by the hair and thrown to the floor. Her daughter had been shoved from the davenport onto the floor. Things had been moved about in the house, and noises in the night made it difficult for them to sleep. The husband, who had not been personally attacked, insisted that his wife and step-daughter were making it up.

When Gertrude and I arrived at the house we found five people waiting for us. Mrs. Smith (not her real name) had shared her experiences and her fears with a few of her neighbors in their rural community, and of course everyone wanted in on the investigation.

Ordinarily, Gertrude and I discouraged group meetings for a number of reasons, primarily for the protection of the family. In this case, however, Mrs. Smith obviously was enjoying her position in the spotlight.

We all sat around a large family dining room table. For almost an hour the group plied us with questions. They were all members of the Catholic faith and had heard of exorcisms, but none of them had ever experienced anything paranormal. They were not only skeptical, but a little frightened. All of them believed that the situation was evil, and that the devil was behind it. This in itself was reason enough to revel in their fear, to be "deliciously" terrified.

As the members of the group began to bond, most of them shared paranormal tales of their own. Mrs. Smith told us that her husband was very angry with her for even talking about the subject. One day while he was screaming at her from the yard as he walked toward his car, the rear window shattered and the pieces of glass fell at his feet. She was certain this was caused by the spirit, but of course he only became more violent in his repudiation of her claims.

After about an hour Mrs. Smith told us that she had learned more about her own Catholic religion and the meaning of its rituals from our conversation than she had learned in a lifetime in her church. Having some knowledge of such rituals, I explained those that pertain to protection from evil spirits, and some of the devices used to exorcise the so-called demons. I also assured her that her visitor was no evil demon, merely a distressed, unhappy spirit trying to reach someone for help.

Gertrude had gone about her usual exploration of the house, inside and out, while I kept the hostess and her inquisitive guests occupied in conversation. She now reported that the spirit was a woman who was, indeed, very upset. The spirit claimed to have been murdered by her husband a few years before, and buried in the yard. Her soul was restless, crying out for a decent Christian burial. She said that her husband, now remarried to the second Mrs. Smith, had told the neighbors that his wife had left him and gone back east to live with relatives.

As we sat around the table talking, Gertrude informed us that the spirit was present, listening to our conversation. At one point a neighbor remarked that she did not believe what she was hearing. She did not believe that the dead were conscious, because the Bible said the dead would be awakened at the judgment day.

Gertrude laughed and informed us that the spirit had said indignantly, "Just wait until you die; you'll find out you're not dead."

We explained to the spirit that she would be much better off going into the light, and that the location of her physical body was not important. We also discussed the impracticality of attempting to pursue this matter with the police. Certainly the husband would not cooperate in digging up his yard. We had no evidence to present to the police.

The spirit was greatly relieved just to be heard and understood. She apologized for the pain she had caused the mother and daughter, but she felt so trapped she had to do something to get help. We explained how she could be free in a happy place. She agreed to leave. As far as we could tell, she left with spirits who came at her request.

A follow-up on this case confirmed our earlier conclusions about Mr. Smith. His wife was not ready to drop the matter. She told him that the psychic had said there was a body buried in their yard — without mentioning, of course, that he had put it there. She asked him to investigate. He became very angry and threatened to have us arrested if we ever came on his land again. This information was conveyed to us by a phone call, and that was the end of that case. We had released a spirit from an intolerable entrapment and considerably mitigated the fears of a number of superstitious people. In fact, we had a very nice note from Mrs. Smith, thanking us for the understanding she had gained about life and death through our visit. She also wanted us to know that no further unpleasant events or manifestations of a spirit visitor had occurred.

In the next chapter we will explore four cases in which the entity seemed to be held to the earth energy by an attachment to a living person. This can be both a good and a very uncomfortable experience for the host. Evidence from our research and from paranormal literature seems to indicate that attachment to a living person is one of the most common reasons for an entity to remain earthbound. In many cases where there has been a powerful love bond between two people, the spirit of the person who dies first will remain with the living partner until death unites them in the spirit world.

CHAPTER 10

Discarnates Held by an Emotional Attachment

Her Pet Was the Victim

The woman in this case was an intellectual in the highest sense of the word. Leila was a university administrator, highly respected for her contributions to the academic world. When she came to me she apologized for harboring any credence in paranormal phenomena. However, knowing my reputation as a parapsychologist, she wanted to ask my advice.

Leila explained that she was very much attached to her cat, which had been with her for almost ten years. During the previous two months the animal had become quite ill on three occasions. Each time she took it to the veterinarian, who could find nothing seriously wrong. The cat quickly recovered in the custody of the hospital and was returned to Leila.

In the course of our conversation Leila admitted that she had been very depressed for a number of months and could not understand why. She wondered if her attitude could possibly have affected the cat.

When I called Gertrude about this one she assured me there was no need to go to Leila's house. She could use her psychic ability to give me the answer to Leila's problem, and since Leila was a good friend of mine, I could simply relay the message to her.

Gertrude then proceeded to relate a most bizarre story which I must confess I was reluctant to tell Leila. She said that Leila had lost a very dear friend in an accident a few months previously. This friend had remained with Leila because she felt safe with her. The death had been so sudden that she was not prepared to die and did not know where to go or what to do. Leila's cat, however, annoyed her. In order to get rid of the cat she had made it ill. Gertrude assured me that the cat would eventually die if it remained in the house with the spirit. She urged me to tell Leila that she must be firm. She must insist that her friend leave her house and go to the light.

The spirit's feeling of being lost and frightened was causing Leila to be depressed, because she was actually picking up or tuning in on the spirit's feelings.

I found it difficult to give this information to my friend. It seemed unlikely that she would be affected so negatively by the death of a friend, and the cat story sounded totally weird. However, she had asked me for help and I did have considerable confidence in Gertrude's ability to "see" things, so I called Leila on the phone and told her exactly what Gertrude had picked up. There was a long pause. I expected her to tell me I was totally wrong. Instead her voice held a note of incredulity as she confirmed Gertrude's statement about the death of her friend. She said she had never connected that death with her own depression, although she admitted that she thought about her friend frequently and wondered why the woman kept coming into her mind. She assured me she had not been affected in that way before, even when members of her own family died.

What really amazed her, however, was the reason given for the cat's illness. Her friend hated cats. When she was alive she always insisted that the cat be put out of the house whenever she came to visit. We discussed how Leila was to handle the situation. She said she was quite up to dealing with it herself, now that she understood the problem.

She called me a few days later to report the results of her efforts. She had explained the facts to her spirit friend, that it was not good for either of them for her to stay any longer. She told her she must move on into the light. While Leila's scientific background made it difficult for her to accept this series of events, she nevertheless had no other explanation. The energy in her house and her own feelings improved dramatically. She assured me that she felt like her normal self again; the depression was totally gone. I saw her often from time to time after that, and the cat remained perfectly well.

A number of interesting questions and observations in the above case merit consideration. The woman in the case was a sophisticated, highly intelligent, retired administrator. She lived in a beautiful home on attractive acreage and enjoyed emeritus status among her colleagues in the community. Her activities included lecturing, numerous social functions, chairing ad hoc committees in various organizations, and so on. In the years I had known her I had never encountered any negative energy around her or from her. She was always enthusiastic about whatever project currently occupied her time.

The depression to which she had succumbed was quite foreign to her nature. This lends credence to the idea that some unusual influence was present in her life at that time. If the analysis of the problem is correct, it illustrates the powerful impact one mind can have on another, even when the individual is totally unaware of the attacking influence.

However, the vulnerability of the victim should never be overlooked. I do not believe an event can occur to any individual without cause, purpose, and a modicum of personal responsibility. Therefore I spent some time with Leila and learned that she was under considerable stress from an elderly relative who had come to live with her. The lady was a partial invalid and required considerable care. On the conscious level Leila was doing a good job of handling this disruption to her previously well-ordered, independent lifestyle.

It doesn't take a professional analyst to conclude that Leila would be struggling with resentment and frustration over her situation. Her personal religious philosophy would lead her to feel guilty about these uncontrollable feelings. These are exactly the sort of emotional conflicts that create stress. Could this be the reason Leila was so vulnerable to the negative energy from her dead friend? We cannot be certain that this is an accurate diagnosis. However, as in all the cases of psychic invasion I have encountered, this one seems to provide additional evidence for such a theory.

This was one of the first cases that Gertrude diagnosed over the phone. Most people with paranormal problems need personal contact with a psychic or the investigator. It serves to give them moral support and confidence in the process. This case proved to me that a good clairvoyant tunes in to the individuals involved, to the problem, and to the solution, from any distance.

An analysis of the *modus operandi* of a psychic might explain this seemingly difficult feat. Research indicates that all activity creates energy patterns. Those patterns are available to a psychic, who tunes in by mental selection. This might be compared to a radio or television set that selects specific sounds and pictures occurring at great distances. An increasing number of clairvoyant counselors serve their clients by telephone rather than in offices. However it may be explained, the fact remains that all knowledge seems to be available to individuals who have this special sensitivity.

This is admittedly a simplistic explanation of a complex subject. Despite all of the research in the last century both in psychology and parapsychology, we are a long way from understanding the role that the conscious and unconscious mind plays in our experiences as human beings.

One other analogy may help take some of the mystery out of the psychic's ability to perceive events and people at various distances. If each individual generates his or her own unique energy vibrations, this could be analogous to the specific frequencies emitted by radio and TV stations, or to the endless individualized cellular phone numbers now in vogue among business people. Instruments invented by human minds can pick up radio signals, or connect with specific telephones, over great distances. Surely it should be possible for a highly sensitive mind to extend its energy to a specific individual's unique energy vibration. This idea is somewhat substantiated by the spontaneous remarks made by many psychics at the beginning of a reading: "Give me a minute to tune in to (or locate) his vibrations."

Dealing with Suicide

The son of one of my very close friends always seemed to attract traumatic events. Chris would go out for an evening and end up in jail for driving while intoxicated. He would go surfing and end up in the hospital with broken ribs. He would find a roommate to share the expenses of his apartment and come home to find some of his property gone, along with the "friend" who still owed him two months' rent. He seemed to have a penchant for attracting friends who either "took him for a ride" or got him into some sort of trouble.

Chris met up with an old school acquaintance. Over a period of several years they became fast friends. Perry, a very lonely man, felt that no one loved him. He had been estranged from his parents since he was a small boy. When he was sixteen they ordered him out of the home because of his lifestyle. Perry often talked about suicide, but Chris always managed to dissuade him and lift his spirits, even though Chris himself had often contemplated suicide.

One night, with a feeling of panic, Chris awoke suddenly. Perry's name flashed through his mind. He was quite certain something had happened to his friend. He was finally able to sleep the balance of the night. In the morning he tried to reach Perry, without success. Later in the day Chris spoke with his mother on the phone. She asked him if he had seen the morning paper. It carried a story of Perry's suicide the previous evening.

From that time on, Chris began to feel very depressed over the death of his friend. He would sit on the edge of his bed, suicidal thoughts crowding his mind. His mother told me about this behavior and asked my advice. Since I knew Chris fairly well, I managed to have a chat with him. I tried to explain what was going on. I told him he must send Perry away to his own energy field; this contact was not good for either of them.

Chris adamantly insisted that he felt Perry was trying to get help from him. Since he loved Perry he could not just coldly reject him and refuse to help. All of my logic had no weight with Chris. He was certain that somehow he could help Perry, and there was no way he would refuse to try. He admitted that as he sat alone thinking of Perry he believed that he was actually communicating with him. He felt Perry's presence and even "heard" his specific thoughts. He said Perry was lonely. His friend missed him and wanted them to be together again. I tried to convince Chris that this could be actually dangerous to him, his health and his welfare. He simply reiterated that if he could help by listening, he could not reject his friend.

About two weeks after our conversation, Chris' mother called to tell me that Chris had been in a car accident. His car had struck a telephone pole but was repairable. Chris came out of the accident with a broken collarbone but was otherwise unharmed. She told me that Chris wanted to talk with me because he was really frightened. He was convinced that Perry had tried to kill him.

I made an appointment with Chris. When he arrived at my office he was considerably shaken up. He assured me what had happened was not his imagination. He had not been drinking. As he was driving his car home something grabbed his steering wheel and turned the car into a telephone pole. He said he tried to control the car but was unable to turn the wheel. It had felt as if it was locked.

We discussed his experience at length. He could not understand why his friend would want to harm him. Chris is a loyal, sensitive and caring person. The idea that someone who loved him could try to kill him was beyond his ability to comprehend. I tried to explain to him that Perry did not think of death as something bad. He probably wanted Chris to share his new-found freedom. He had discovered that there was no such thing as death, and wanted them to be together to share this experience. I pointed out to him that he also had often thought of suicide, for he considered his own life a disaster. Since Perry was in a position to be aware of Chris' wish to be free of his problems, he considered death a logical, practical solution. Perhaps, to his way of thinking, he would be doing Chris a favor by liberating him from the drudgery of his earth life.

Chris said that he now understood what I had tried to tell him. He had given it considerable thought and decided he was not ready to leave. He had things to do in his life that now took on a new importance. We discussed how he could approach Perry in a loving way and make it very clear that he was not ready to die. I explained to Chris how important it was that he urge Perry to leave the earth plane and move into the light.

I did not hear from him for about two weeks. Then his mother called to relay his message to me. Chris wanted me to know that the depression was totally gone, and so was Perry. Their parting had been sad but very real to him, and he had a more positive feeling about himself. His mother told me she could scarcely believe the change in him and in his attitude.

This experience occurred a number of years ago. Chris has gone on to make a name for himself in the literary world. Unlike many creative people he will never be an extroverted individual. His life is totally engrossed in his writing. He does not consider himself to be psychic, yet he seems to be the recipient of inspirational ideas. His mother insists he has always had a second sense about things.

In retrospect, many incidents in our lives seem to take on special significance. Chris's life was changed following his experience. Did Perry, from his vantage point, create a situation out of which

Chris would discover a reason to live? Or was the whole scenario a cerebral creation of Chris's mind, resulting from his grief over the loss of a friend? Or was it in the destiny pattern Chris had long ago created to motivate him toward his goals? A fourth possibility will come to the minds of many New Age devotees. If Chris had a guardian angel, or spirit guide, did that entity orchestrate the entire experience for Chris' benefit? As human beings we are all curious about the real reason for life and events, but in the long run the precise answer really is not so important. The marked change and new purposefulness in Chris' life verifies the value of the experience. All of the above postulates may be operating, or there may be more we have not considered. As we search for these answers, life becomes an increasingly challenging experience.

The Whistling Sister

Over the years I have taught many classes in the development of intuitive abilities. In one such class two of the students were sisters. They were said to possess remarkable psychic gifts, and other members of the class were delighted when they decided to join us. Patsy and Eva had established a reputation among their friends for their skill at "table-tipping." They would sit on opposite sides of a table and touch the top of the table lightly with their fingers. The table would shake, lift on one side, and occasionally levitate. Questions could be asked of the table; it would rise on one side and tap the floor, once for "yes," twice for "no."

On their first evening with the group we also had another newcomer, a client of mine who was deeply interested in parapsychology. Jack had never acknowledged his own psychic ability, but he was very aware of the many times in his life when he "knew" things before they happened. He had come to me as a client to explore his ability, determine why he had it, and learn if there was something he was supposed to do with it.

Shortly after we began working together Jack discovered that on certain occasions he could actually "see" spirit forms. On one occasion he visited a prospective client. He arrived as the family was preparing to take an elderly relative to a mental institution because of her delusional behavior. As he entered the room he was amazed to see a rather ugly spirit form overlapping her body. To everyone's astonishment the elderly lady pointed her finger angrily at Jack and almost screamed at him, "Don't you come near me. You get out of here! She is mine and I'm not leaving her."

The experience shook him, but he felt helpless to interfere in any way. He was there on real estate business, and was quite certain that the family would not accept what he had seen as valid. They would simply interpret the old woman's outburst as further evidence of her delusions, and think he was weird if he mentioned the spirit form. This new paranormal ability troubled him, and he wondered what he was supposed to do with it. From that time on he often saw spirit forms around people. He could also see the auric force field that surrounds most people. I could never get away with declaring I felt fine if that was not true. He would laugh and tell me where I was hurting.

At the particular meeting I mentioned above, an interesting experience occurred. The class was eagerly awaiting Patsy and Eva's table-tipping demonstration. Unfortunately, the hostess did not own a card table. I suggested that they use the piano bench, and they agreed. Sitting on opposite sides of the bench, they had barely touched its surface when it began to rock forcefully back and forth, as if it was dancing. The sisters had trouble trying to keep their fingers on its surface; often there was space between their hands and the bench. The class laughed with delight. I finally asked them to stop because I thought such violent banging around would damage the bench.

During this performance Jack dropped down beside me and whispered, "I can see who is moving the bench." I asked him to share it with the group, but he declined. He insisted everyone would laugh at him. However, after the meeting was formally over and we had discussed the lesson for the evening he felt much more comfortable. Realizing that these people would accept his experience, he agreed to share what he had seen.

He described a young girl, including her clothes and her tight-fitting hat, and estimated her age at about seventeen. The sisters gasped. Patsy shouted, "My God, that sounds like Ida, our sister! She died when she was almost eighteen." Jack went on to say that after moving the bench about, she sat on the floor cross-legged and whistled. Then she quoted an old-fashioned ditty that went something like this: "Whistling girls and cackling hens always come to no good ends."

Jack's revelation shocked the sisters. They explained that when Ida was a young girl she loved to whistle. Their mother repeatedly told her that whistling was not lady-like. She told Ida not to whistle, and quoted that rhyme to her. In addition they remembered that she habitually sat cross-legged on the floor. Their mother also considered this to be very unladylike behavior. Psychic as they were, neither sister had ever suspected that Ida was the spirit who tipped tables for them when people wanted to be amused by this phenomenon.

Needless to say, the class was delighted. The incident provided rather substantial evidence that, first, table-tipping is not produced solely by the kinetic energy of the persons touching the table and, second, that intelligent personalities in the other dimension could and did interact in this way with people they loved.

At the time of this experience I was quite unsophisticated in the art of sending spirits to the light. Since Ida seemed to be enjoying the interaction with her sisters, and they with her, I made no attempt to talk her into leaving. We discovered that she was quite willing to answer questions by tapping yes and no answers with the table. The class enjoyed this exercise. Jack was not a regular member of the class, so he was not there to have direct communication with her. However, a few months later she informed us, through another visiting psychic, that she had learned that she must move on in order to develop her "soul." She would not see us again. From that time on, Patsy and Eva were unable to tip tables.

In all my years of research, even the most gifted psychics communicated telepathically. Although they almost never "saw" spirits, they somehow "knew" what they looked like and could describe them. Jack was one of the few gifted sensitives who apparently observed a spirit projected out in front of him. He explained that although he could see through them, the spirits were very clear, recognizable in details such as features, clothing, and size. The conversations were accomplished telepathically; he did not hear an audible voice. However, audible sounds have been recorded on rare occasions involving considerable negative emotion, such as in the case recorded in chapter 3, entitled "Double Trouble."

My experience with Patsy, Eva, and Ida helped me to accept the possibility that table-tipping, ouija boards, even pendulums were, at least sometimes, moved by the energy generated by discarnate beings. Most of my psychological colleagues were convinced these phenomena were produced by kinetic energy generated by a disturbed individual. This theory accounts for poltergeist activity, a phenomenon that seems to be associated with troubled adolescents. While that observation has merit, I prefer another explanation. Adolescents, being very emotional, attract discarnate entities who can express themselves through the disturbed young person. Since the mind has the power to create its own reality, we have no way at the present time to prove any theory propounded to explain paranormal phenomena. It may very well be that there is actually more than one explanation. In the case of pendulums, for example, the most widely accepted theory is that the mind of the person holding the pendulum directs its swing from the unconscious. This is not to say that individuals who believe a spirit helper is directing the answers are wrong. We simply do not know.

Albert's Playmate

Many children have imaginary playmates. One wonders how many of them might actually be spirit companions, visible because the children have not been taught that such experiences are impossible. One of the saddest cases I have encountered in my investigations involved a young man who came to me for help. Albert was in his late twenties and worked as a laborer for a construction company. When he came to my house I wanted to ask him to remove his shoes, for they were almost encrusted with mud. His clothes were rumpled and sweaty. I tried to hide my feelings and invited him to sit on my davenport. I suppose the fact that he was the nephew of a very close friend encouraged me to be a little more accepting. At any rate, the following story describes his dilemma.

One Sunday, while sitting in church, Albert suddenly felt himself up at the podium, standing beside the minister. This was such a shock to him that he dropped his program. From the podium he saw the paper slip out of his hand. His first thought was that he was dead, but his body looked quite alive as it sat there in the pew. Then he thought, "If I look over the shoulder of the minister and read his notes, and then he says what I have just read, I will know I am really up here." So he moved closer, looked over the minister's shoulder, read the notes, and listened. Sure enough the words came out of the minister's mouth just as he had read them seconds before. A sense of sheer panic swept over him. The next instant he was back in his body, looking up at the minister.

This experience so unnerved him that he told his uncle, a gifted psychic who bore the brunt of the family's jokes. He knew his uncle would not laugh at his experience, and perhaps could help him understand it. Instead, his uncle insisted that he see me. We discussed his experience. I asked him if he had ever had any other paranormal encounters of any kind, and he told me the following story.

When he was a very young boy he used to play in the barn on his parents' farm. His father set aside one corner for him. On a makeshift table Albert laid out a miniature farm. He made buildings and collected animals for this play farm, and spent many hours playing there. What he did not tell anyone was that an old man was always with him, helping him build the things he made. His parents often commented on the skill he displayed for such a young boy. He still did not tell them about the old man. This play world lasted for about two years. Albert's model was often displayed for admiring relatives and friends.

One day when he was about seven, he and his mother were talking about his absorption in his project. He decided to tell her about his old friend. When he described the old man his mother burst into tears, and forbade him to ever speak of it again. She told him he was lying and a very bad boy to make up such stories. His father then confronted him and told him that he had described his mother's father, who had died a number of years before. He accused the boy of having seen a photograph of the old man. He said he would punish his son severely if he ever mentioned the matter again.

Albert had never, to his knowledge, seen his grandfather's photograph, but he did know what he was seeing in the barn. The old man talked with him, helped him, and played with him. A few days later he tried again to talk with his mother about it. He felt he had to make her understand that he was not lying or trying to hurt her. Again she broke into violent weeping, accused him of lying, and told his father. Albert's father horse-whipped him and locked him in his room. He was told that he could not come out until he admitted to his mother that he was lying.

He stayed in his room for many hours. He tried to understand the reactions of his parents and decide what he should do. He ended up apologizing to his mother and totally destroying his model farm. He decided that there was something very wrong with his mind, and that he was some sort of an inferior human being. From that day on he felt like an outcast. He believed that if anyone knew about his experience they would summarily reject him.

Although Albert was a very intelligent young man, he always sought jobs that would allow him to go unnoticed in any way. When the experience in the church occurred, it was as if a door long-closed had been opened again. I spent considerable time with Albert and was successful in giving him back to himself. We worked in an altered state so that he could clearly see the value of his psychic gift, and the reason his parents had been so upset. He realized that they had no knowledge of paranormal phenomena and were genuinely concerned about the welfare of their son. Indeed, they believed that he might have been possessed by the devil. In an altered state he accepted his special gift. He was grateful that the door had been opened again, for it gave him a new image of himself. In addition, he realized that he was not in the kind of work he should be doing.

A follow-up on Albert six months later found him well-dressed, confident, and holding a responsible job with the same construction company. He was no longer digging ditches. He was in an office of his own, making administrative decisions for his company.

Why had this grandfather come, in spirit, to play with his grandson? An emotional attachment would seem to be the logical answer, but in life he had never known the boy. Was the purpose of his contact to develop Albert's psychic ability? Surely he would have known that the experience would create real problems for the boy. And what caused Albert to leave his body in church? Was some wiser part of himself taking over at that point, creating a situation in which he would discover himself and take himself out of the prison he had created as a result of his anger and fear? Many fascinating questions remain unanswered in such cases. If the individual is inclined to seek his own answers, past-life regression therapy can often shed light on the purpose of life's events. There is mounting evidence that every experience has a cause and a purpose. In retrospect, with an in-depth analysis, many of these puzzling questions can be answered on an individual basis, for the reasons are almost certain to be different for each person involved.

In many cases a discarnate may wander about in a lost state for a considerable length of time, trying in one way or another to get the attention of someone who might help him or her. Two distinctly different cases will be presented in the next chapter. The first deals with an angry young man determined to make someone listen to him. The second case involves a very young boy, totally unaware of where he is or what has happened to him. This boy reaches out for help wherever he sees the special light that indicates a sensitive person.

CHAPTER 11

Desperate Entities
Seek Help

Terror at Night

Seldom have I seen a young woman so terrified. Helen's experiences were so bizarre that she was afraid to tell her parents. She feared they would believe she was crazy and send her to a hospital. In fact, she was not at all sure they would not be right. Certainly something was wrong with her mind. She finally confided in her closest friend, Margaret, the daughter of one of my clients. Margaret assured Helen that her mother knew someone who could help her. Still afraid to tell her parents, Helen asked Margaret's mother to bring her to my house.

After the appointment was made I called Gertrude and gave her the story as Helen had related it to me. This case was one of our first, and Gertrude was still skeptical of her own abilities as an exorcist. She felt more comfortable when she had advance information about a case. This gave her time to be quiet and concentrate on the situation. She always received instructions about how to help the person involved, but she was reluctant to tell me about it because she did not understand what she was doing. She often felt foolish performing some of the rituals she was instructed to perform. However, as time went on and we continued to get positive results, we both came to feel less "silly" about some of the things we did.

Helen's story began one night after she had gone to bed. As she was drifting off to sleep she suddenly felt an eerie sensation of not being alone. She tried to raise her head to look around; to her horror, she was unable to move. Try as she would, she could not move her body at all. She felt as though she were paralyzed. She tried to scream for help, but was unable to make a sound. After a few minutes the sensation subsided and she was able to get out of bed. As she started for her parent's room she stopped. What would she tell them? She realized how absurd her story would sound. They would just tell her she had been having a nightmare. She returned to her bed and lay in fear for a short time before finally falling asleep.

This same scenario was repeated a number of times over a period of two weeks. Then one night as she lay in this state of paralysis, she thought someone spoke to her. The voice said, "Speak to me, speak to me." She opened her eyes. A young man knelt by her bed, looking at her. Again she tried to scream for help, but only a low moan came from her throat. She closed her eyes for a few seconds; when she opened them again the apparition was gone. On the morning after this experience she confided in her friend Margaret, and two days later they came to Riverside for help.

When they arrived Gertrude was already there. Following introductions the first thing I heard was Gertrude saying, "Well, I am sorry, young man, but I AM going to do something about this." She then explained that an angry spirit was present. The moment he saw her he said, "You stay out of this. She is mine and you can't make me leave her."

Gertrude instructed Helen to stand in the middle of the floor. She then proceeded to walk around her three times, sprinkling a combination of herbs on my carpet. I was not at all sure I could go for that hocus pocus ritual, but I decided it was just for show and that Gertrude was creating an energy shield around Helen. Whatever the explanation, it seemed to work. The angry spirit was quite upset. He told Gertrude he did not know what she had done, but he could not get to Helen anymore.

I gave the discarnate visitor a nice lecture on what he could do to be free of this entrapment, and how he could call for help in his dimension and find peace of mind. He broke in and said to Gertrude, "Will you tell that bitch to shut up so I can think?" After giving him a few seconds to think, I ventured a second attempt. The following conversation ensued, Gertrude feeding me his responses to my remarks.

"There are people in your dimension who will help you if you will just ask. You must have relatives who have gone before you, maybe a grandmother or grandfather —"

He broke in indignantly. "I never had any truck with my relatives when I was on earth. I'm not about to start over here."

"Well, then, perhaps you had a friend who died before you did who could come to help you."

As I finished this sentence, Gertrude broke in to tell us that another spirit had come into the room. He slapped our spirit on the back and said, "Ralph, you old son-of-a-gun, what kind of a mess have you got yourself in now?"

Ralph replied, "I just wanted to talk with this girl."

"Don't you know you can't mess around with a young girl and not get into trouble?"

"But I only wanted to talk with her. She can hear me. Nobody else could."

At this point my curiosity took over and I decided to attempt a question. I asked Ralph how he was able to paralyze Helen when she was in her bed. He said, "Oh, that was easy. I used to be a boxer and I knew the spot in her neck to press." I never did know whether this answer had any validity or not. It did not seem important enough to investigate, but that was his explanation.

Gertrude reported that the two spirits were conversing. After a few seconds she reported that Ralph's friend had convinced him that he could take him to a place where this would all be explained. He would not have to stay earthbound any longer. Ralph seemed satisfied that he could trust his friend, and they both left.

The entire encounter lasted approximately half an hour. We all felt relieved that Ralph had responded so positively to our help. We assured Helen that she would no longer be troubled by this young man. In his desperation he had sought help from her because she was psychic. She had not known about her gift, so we spent another hour talking with her about how she could use her sensitivity in a positive way in her life.

A follow-up on this case confirmed our prognosis. Helen was never troubled again.

Who Caused Her Heart Attack?

The following case is an excellent example of the power of fear in spirit encounters. The lady who called me was a registered nurse, trained to remain calm and controlled in emergencies. Over the phone she assured me that she was not easily frightened, but her experience had left her in a state of panic. She begged me to believe her, and to come without delay to her house.

When we arrived she gave us more details of her experience. As she was sitting reading, someone or "some thing" had put pressure on her foot and pushed it down flat on the floor. It was an unmistakable act and gave her what she thought was a heart attack. The physical symptoms were so real that her daughter rushed her to the hospital. Tests were made, but no pathology was found, and as the pain had totally subsided she returned home.

Other strange things which she had ignored or considered unimportant now began to take on some significance. Strange noises had been heard in the house, objects seemed to have been moved, and in one particular area of her living room she had experienced a sense of discomfort strong enough to give her "goose bumps." She had assured herself that these manifestations were merely a figment of her imagination — until her foot was forced to the floor.

As Gertrude walked through the house she very quickly picked up the energy of the invisible visitor. It was the spirit of a small, lost, frightened boy. He recognized the sensitivity of this lady and was trying to make contact with her to ask for her help.

It was interesting to all of us that Gertrude described the previous tenant of the house as a young girl experimenting with witchcraft. She used to set up a makeshift altar in the area of the room that caused our client to feel so uncomfortable, light a candle, and invoke the spirits to come to her. The little lost spirit was drawn to her ritual. When she moved out of the house he was left behind. He did not know where to go, but felt reasonably safe in the area to which he had been attracted. Gertrude explained that the spirit told her he had tried many times to get help, but could never find anyone who would listen to him. The young lady with her candle had seemed like the answer, since she was inviting a visitation. However, he had been disappointed again, for she was not even aware of his presence. He said he was sorry he had frightened our client, but he could tell by her "light" that she was a kind person and would be aware of him.

As Gertrude described the unhappy state of this child spirit, we all felt compassion for him. Our client then asked why, if he was such a good little spirit, he had caused her to have a heart attack. Gertrude told her that it had been her own fear that had caused the pain in her chest. She was able to accept that explanation.

We then spent a brief time talking with the young spirit and helping him to understand that there was a better place for him. He need only ask for help from someone in his dimension and it would be there. He thanked us for our help. Gertrude told us that two spirits appeared and took charge of him. He left with them.

The woman and her daughter had many questions about their experience, for the daughter had also been uncomfortably aware of something in the house which she could not explain. She had not mentioned it to her mother for fear of being ridiculed, so she had no idea that her mother was having the same feelings. Both were open-minded and totally convinced of the validity of their experiences. When they realized we would understand and not make light of their story, they urged us to stay and answer their questions about the phenomena they had encountered. We were always willing to accommodate clients in this way. It gave us an opportunity to help people understand the reality of the other dimension and the close connection that exists between the two worlds.

The mother was especially fascinated and asked us many questions. In her role as a nurse she had encountered experiences with her patients that now had new meaning for her. It was almost midnight when we left the two women. We felt it had been one of our happier experiences, a problem easily resolved. A follow-up confirmed our expectations. They had no further encounters with the spirit.

These cases occurred almost twenty years ago. Had they been isolated experiences, we could have summarily dismissed them on the grounds of their paranormal nature. The only evidence of their validity, if it can be called evidence, lies in the fact that the subjects totally recovered from their symptoms. Could there be other explanations for their recovery? The most obvious and most widely accepted by the scientific community postulates that their recovery was simply the result of their belief. In other words, my colleague and I were successful in selling them a new belief system to replace their fears.

This explanation has considerable merit. We did indeed give them a new belief system. However, it was based on more than a fanciful fabrication of the psychic. In many of our cases the individuals under attack had called in other so-called specialists, including psychologists, ministers, exorcists, priests and psychics, with no positive results. We listened to many accounts of their attempts to solve these paranormal problems. The psychologists used reconditioning measures, logic, and at times committed the "possessed" person to a mental institution. Ministers were for the most part limited to prayers and exhortations which generally proved ineffective. Exorcists approached most cases with the premise that the offending spirit was the devil or one of his henchmen, and must be forced out in the name of God or Jesus Christ. Priests used exorcism as their primary weapon. The skill of the psychic determined whether or not they were successful. We found that many psychics were frightened by the manifestations they encountered, as described in chapter 3's "Double Trouble." None of these approaches worked, even though the victims believed they were calling on people with skill in solving such problems. Therefore it seems logical to assume that belief alone is not powerful enough to free victims of psychic harassment.

Throughout this century, openminded individuals have had to work incognito in the paranormal field to maintain their public, professional image. Many years ago I heard a talk by Baroness Lotte Von Strahl, the famous German clairvoyant who fled with her husband to England and then Hollywood to escape Hitler's persecution. She became famous in Southern California, and her advice was sought by many of Hollywood's greatest. For a period of time she worked in a mental institution as a consultant to a psychiatrist who would not allow his name to be used. Her assignment was to tell him which patients were really mentally disturbed, and which were clairvoyant and misdiagnosed.

Unfortunately, as a result of our cultural non-belief in the paranormal field, many gifted people are pronounced mentally ill. Psychological personality profiles measure a person's sanity by the response to such questions as, "Do you ever hear voices?" If the answer is "yes," the assumption made is that the subject is not in touch with reality. Is it any wonder that people hide their "hunches?" Should they be gifted enough to have precognitive insight they assume their minds are deranged. Having made that diagnosis of themselves, they are self-condemned to a life of deception and secrecy. They believe that if anyone knew their horrible secret, they would be considered unacceptable by society.

If any of our readers believe this is an exaggerated statement, let me assure them it is not. I have listened to hundreds of clients who share their psychic experiences with me AFTER they discover I will understand and accept as valid the stories they tell me. In most cases they have never shared their experiences with anyone else. Many clients who seek my help have been in traditional therapy. They tell me that they have never shared their experiences with their "shrink" for fear of being diagnosed as abnormal.

Dramatic changes have occurred in the last few years. I now know of many traditional psychotherapists who have accepted the validity of humankind's spiritual nature, and of our capacity to move into an exciting new dimension of reality. With this greater understanding and acceptance, many of our current personal and social problems can be resolved.

When Gertrude and I were working with these problems I was convinced that it was a universal phenomena that needed to be addressed. At that time, however, our work was still considered beyond the notice of educated people, who dealt only with facts that could be measured and substantiated. It is personally gratifying to read of the ever-increasing number of professionals who are either including what is now termed "invasion" in their practices, or in some cases specializing in this field.

At this point I am reminded of a statement made by the late Dr. Gardner Murphy. Dr. Murphy headed the research division of the Menninger Foundation for many years. Upon his retirement, he devoted his full attention to psychical research. In the Sunday supplement of a Los Angeles newspaper a number of years ago, he said that anyone who did not accept the findings in the field of parapsychology was either ignorant or prejudiced, since the evidence was incontrovertible.

A list of the purposes for which entities have discourse with mortals would not be complete without the inclusion of the many gifts they have brought to humanity through this type of communication. In the next chapter I shall depart from my presentation of first-hand experiences, and present a few of the spectacular cases noted and reported in the literature of the paranormal.

CHAPTER 12

Entities Who Return to Help and Share Talents

If intelligent beings exist in another dimension, why have they not helped humanity, rather than communicating the trivia one encounters at so many seances? This question is frequently directed to parapsychologists and metaphysicians who support the hypothesis that there is intelligent communication between the physical and spiritual world.

The answer is that these beings do help, and have offered such help over the centuries. Their contact takes many forms, from dreams to visions. Perhaps the most common form of communication is better known by the term "intuition." In literature we often encounter the phrase, "Something spoke to me." It is not at all uncommon to hear inventors, artists, writers, and scientists admit that often, when they are "stuck" in a project, something tells their minds what to do.

Although no clear-cut evidence identifies the source of the intuition, inspiration, hunch, insight, or whatever one wishes to call it, the phenomenon seems to fall into two somewhat different categories. In the first case, an idea appears to come from a storehouse of knowledge that is already "there." In the second category, some type of information seems to be individualized to meet the needs of the occasion or the person.

Jonas Salk

Because of his international reputation Jonas E. Salk, the creator of a vaccine for the relief of Infantile Paralysis, provides an outstanding example of a recipient of information of which he had no previous knowledge. He once said, "The answer pre-exists; the problem is to formulate the correct question."[1]

Frederick August Kekule

Perhaps one of the most significant examples of information attributed to the other dimension is the Benzine Ring. The famous German Chemist, Frederick August Kekule, made far-reaching contributions to an understanding of carbon compounds. In spite of many hours of experimentation and research, he was still puzzled. Then he was given a dream in which he saw a field of dancing carbon atoms. The atoms arranged themselves into a snake that grabbed its tail, forming a circle. That was the secret he sought. Based on his dream, he set forth the essential features of his famous doctrine of the linking of atoms. In 1865 he formulated his "closed chain" or "ring" theory of the constitution of benzine, which was called by his colleagues the "most brilliant piece of prediction to be found in the whole range of organic chemistry." Professor F. R. Japp, delivering a Kekule memorial lecture in 1898, stated that three-fourths of modern organic chemistry is directly or indirectly the product of Kekule's benzine theory.[2]

Most biographies of this great discoverer do not mention the dream that gave him the key to the benzine ring. His biographers, as well as his fellow scientists, thought him slightly unbalanced. However, the significance of his contribution could not be ignored, so they considered him an eccentric.

The key factors behind Kekule's theory were unknown in the scientific world at that time. What was the origin of the revelation that led to this significant discovery? Do all discoveries or so-called inventions exist in some sort of a universal bank of knowledge, waiting for a sensitive to bring them into the physical world?

Elias Howe

Another invention that resulted from a dream was the sewing machine. Elias Howe worked for years to invent a lock stitch for his machine, but success eluded him. Then he had a dream in which he was captured by a primitive tribe of native Africans. He was brought before their chief, who commanded him to complete his machine or be killed. In the dream he could not find a solution, and was led to his execution between two rows of natives carrying spears. As he walked along he noted an eye-shaped hole in the tips of the spears. He awoke with the clear realization that he had been putting the hole in the shank of the needle, when it really needed to go in the tip, as he had been shown in the dream. With this design change the sewing machine was born.[3]

Cuneiform Deciphered

Still another example of information coming through a dream appears the case of the obscure languages of Assyria, Babylonia and Persia. Writing from these cultures was available to scholars, but it consisted of a strange combination of wedge-shaped figures that defied translation for years, despite the combined efforts of language scholars. One such scholar, Professor Herman Hilprecht of the University of Pennsylvania, went to sleep one night with the problem on his mind, and a powerful desire to know the key to these hidden languages. He had a vivid dream in which a Sumerian priest leaned over him and spoke in his ear, telling him the key to cuneiform.

This information, as well as many other examples of mystical experiences, will not be found in standard encyclopedias. The story was illustrated in a collection of strange experiences published a number of years ago.[4]

Hindu Goddess Informs Mathematician

Srinivasa Ramanujan was a great Indian mathematician. He worked on the theory of numbers, the theory of partitions, and the theory of continued fractions. He attributed his many formulas to the Hindu goddess Namakkal. She came to him in dreams when he was ready for a new formula.[5]

Dmitri Mendelyev, Another Dreamer

Dmitri Ivanovich Mendelyev, the Russian chemist and inventor, gave us the Periodic Table of Elements. He was awarded the Davey Medal of the Royal Society in 1882, and received his Copley medal in 1905. He was considered to be one of the greatest teachers of his time.[6]

Writers Who Were Inspired

The German poet Johann Wolfgang von Goethe said of one of his writings, "I wrote the book almost unconsciously, like a somnambulist, and was amazed when I realized what I had done."[7]

The English poet Percy Shelley once declared that "One after another of the greatest writers, poets, and artists confirm the fact that their work comes from beyond the threshold of consciousness."[8]

Henry Wadsworth Longfellow describes his experience in a hypnagogic state. "New thoughts were running in my mind, and I got up to add them to the ballad. I felt pleased with the ballad. It hardly cost me any effort. It did not come into my mind in lines, but by stanzas."[9]

Three Scientists Who Tuned In

Rene Descartes, Nikola Tesla, and Albert Einstein changed the world as they found it, and all claimed intuitive guidance.

As a young man, Descartes dreamed of changing the world through the use of the mind. He believed that his purpose in life was to reform knowledge and unify the sciences. To a large extent he accomplished just that, for he demonstrated for all time that knowledge comes from a non-rational means of knowing. It is a sad commentary on our society that, while his ideas changed the face of modern thinking, the source of his wisdom was ridiculed and ignored.[10]

Few people are familiar with the life and accomplishments of Nikola Tesla, yet our everyday lives would not be the same without his inventions. Electrical currents used in medicine and industry, radio-controlled vehicles, and wireless power are just three of his beneficial discoveries. His ideas came in flashes and dreams. Fortunately he kept careful notes of his intuitive flashes. Current schools of creative mind training are based on his ideas. As has happened to many inspired thinkers, Tesla was ridiculed by his contemporaries and died penniless and bitter.[11]

Albert Einstein's work is too familiar to discuss here, expect to point out that, like many people who have contributed to society, he received his information intuitively.[12]

Musicians Respond to Guidance

The number of musicians who claim information from an outside source is legion. All of their claims were similar: they "heard" the music in their minds. Strauss, Puccini, Brahms, Tchaikovsky, Beethoven — all claimed that their music was inspired by some energy that came to them without their conscious effort. All they had to do was listen. The inspiration often came in a dream.

Richard Strauss expressed it well when he said, "While the ideas were flowing in upon me — the entire musical, measure by measure — it seemed to me that I was dictated to by two wholly different entities." Puccini, in describing how he wrote *Madame Butterfly*, said, "The music of this opera was dictated to me by God."[13]

Both Brahms and Beethoven pointed out that certain inspirations seemed to come from some place other than what they thought of as themselves.[14] Tchaikovsky explained that the germ of a future composition came suddenly and unexpectedly and took root with extraordinary force and rapidity.[15]

Inventor Follows His Hunches

One of my very close friends has been an inventor all of his life. He created everything from miniature musical toys that play on true pitch, to the most complicated miniature machines, to sophisticated prostheses for the replacement of hands and legs. For many years he was an engineer in one of the largest toy companies in the United States. His wife, who was very interested in parapsychology, constantly attempted to draw him into conversations with the implication that he was psychic. He would have none of it, and often made fun of her for her ignorance and superstition. The rest of the family and his friends wisely avoided the subject in his presence.

One day he was having lunch at our house. I had a strong feeling that at long last I could approach him on the subject, so I asked a rather non-threatening question. "I have always been curious about where you get your ideas. Can you tell me how you dream up all of the things you invent?"

His answer, and his attitude, surprised me. He became very serious and looked pensive for a few moments. Then, with a heavy sigh, he said, "I really don't know. Ideas come into my head as a complete formula or design. If I follow them exactly they always turn out successfully. But if I think I can improve on an idea and make changes, it never seems to work."

I could not resist saying, with a laugh, "And you say you are not psychic!" We all laughed and left it at that, but in the years since that conversation he has stopped ridiculing paranormal explanations.

Personalized Guidance

The second type of communication seems to be personalized to suit the recipient's immediate need. A surgeon friend once told me that although he seldom admitted it, when he went into surgery he often felt a presence beside him, especially if the case was difficult or complicated. Something guided his hands. Whenever this occurred the surgery always went smoothly and came to a successful conclusion.

Public Speaker

Chauncey H. Depew, lawyer, politician, and New York State senator, was famous for his oratory. A compilation of his speeches fills twelve volumes. He was selected to give the nomination speech for Roosevelt. According to his report he was given the entire speech in a dream.[16]

Edgar Cayce

No account of information gained clairvoyantly would be complete without including the famous Edgar Cayce. One of my skeptical friends read a book about his life and the readings he gave for people. She remarked that the story was good fiction, but couldn't be true. The fact remains that it IS true. Cayce was probably the greatest psychic in this century.

He was a highly successful professional photographer, Bible student, Sunday School teacher, and devoted family man. Then life changed dramatically for him. He began working in an altered state. While in a trance he gave psychic readings for hundreds of people with both physical and emotional problems. His wife sat by his side as he gave instructions for treatment.

For many years he voluntarily held two sessions each day, and left over 50,000 typewritten pages of stenographic transcripts. A foundation named after him carries on his work. Many of the treatments he prescribed are now being used by medical science, although they were unknown at the time he described them.

He was totally unaware of the information that came through him when he was in trance. After a number of years he began getting readings that attributed the problem to a past life. This disturbed him very much, for he believed that reincarnation was contrary to his Christian beliefs. He determined that he would no longer give the readings, for they could not be good. A difficult period in his life followed this decision. His health suffered, and strange occurrences disrupted his life and work.

He was impressed with a feeling that his problems were the result of his refusing to continue with his psychic work. He became convinced that he had been mistaken, that his work was spiritually inspired, and that he must continue with it, which he did.

Thus began many years of giving readings for people from all over the globe. Those readings have been catalogued by topic on over 200,000 index cards. It may be that no other psychic has been the subject of as many books as this man. His readings included many predictions about coming world events, some of which have already materialized, such as the end of Communism in Russia and an alliance of that country with the United States.[17]

There is no way in which the work of this man can be discounted. It speaks for itself in the undeniable facts that came from his lips while he was in a trance. His case could be explained by either of the previous hypotheses. In his trance state he could have been in touch with a universal bank of knowledge. However, since he was not conscious, how did he identify people who sometimes lived on the opposite side of the world, and bring in the information each of his clients required?

The other explanation fits neatly into any belief system that includes a hierarchy of celestial beings. These beings may never have inhabited physical forms, or may be the spirits of former earth dwellers. In either event they collaborate to assist humanity in its spiritual journey. Individuals with clairvoyant ability receive assistance from this hierarchy in using their gift to help other human beings. In the case of Edgar Cayce, one can speculate that he entered this incarnation with a destiny to mitigate human suffering, and was granted the assistance of one or more spiritual beings to accomplish his purpose.

For those readers who find this idea fanciful and unsubstantiated, some of the recent books on past-life regression therapy are recommended. Hundreds of clients in psychotherapy are resolving long-standing emotional and physical problems using an altered state of consciousness. Through conscious contact with the client, intelligent spiritual beings communicate practical information appropriate to each individual's problem, whatever it may be. This phenomenon is now too common to be dismissed summarily, especially in light of the fact that the success rate is impressively high.

The saga of Edgar Cayce must be considered an outstanding example of the help extended to mortals by intelligent beings who return to the earth plane for the purpose of imparting useful information.

What is the Source of Personal Guidance?

Another common type of communication supports the belief that every person has a spirit guide. Such experiences could be explained as a tuning-in to events that are in some sort of a complex universal blueprint. In other words, the patterns of coming events have already been determined, and a sensitive person merely picks up information in advance of the occurrence. This theory, of course, is in conflict with the idea of free will. In reality, perhaps free will does not consist of choosing events, but of choosing how we handle those events. Many metaphysicians hold this view, and evidence from past-life regression therapy supports it to some extent. Examples of the communication to which I refer include people who believe they are "in tune" with the Source of all knowledge, as well as people who are totally unaware of any such possibility. Many incidents have been recorded of people who are warned of danger and subsequently escape accidents. A common example is the person who has a hunch not to travel on a train, airplane, or ship. The person stays home, and the vehicle is wrecked. This is often a one-time experience. Such people make no claim to being psychic, nor are they aware of undergoing any similar experiences.

Other individuals believe that being aware of and sensitive to help or guidance from some intelligence outside of the self can enhance life. I happen to belong to this group. Over the many years I have been "directed" to action hundreds of times. These directions have kept me from missing trains and planes, and from undergoing unpleasant experiences. I would like to share two events that demonstrate my belief. In neither case is there any way I could have received the information through normal channels.

In the first instance, I was arriving home from the office. As I drove up to my house that "voice" in my mind said, "Park your car in front." Since my garage was a short distance from the house, I always drove into the garage on arrival so I would not have to go out later, after dark, and put the car away. However, I never ignore that "voice." I parked in front, wondering why. Approximately two hours later, as I sat at my typewriter, I heard the pounding of rain on the roof. It was so loud and continued for so long that I finally went to the window and looked out. To my amazement, the entire back yard was a lake, the water held in by a large retaining wall around the condominium. My house was in the last row next to the wall. Workers, up to their knees in water, were trying to make an outlet in the wall to drain off the water. My car was inundated up to the doors. Since there was nothing to be done at the moment I returned to my typewriter.

A few hours later the flooding had been reduced to mud puddles. I went to the garage and found that the water had raced through in such force that all of the bottles, boxes and tools stored in the garage had been washed into the middle. I stood there full of gratitude that I had been spared the experience of dragging all of those objects out from under my car, which is where they would have lodged had it been parked there. The thought came to me: "Who knew that we were going to have a flood? Did an intelligent entity assigned to help me give me the information, or did I pick it up from some sort of an energy pattern 'out there?'"

The second incident occurred shortly after we had organized a psi association. The first speaker was scheduled to come from Los Angeles to speak in one of the elementary schools. On the day of the lecture I was in my kitchen starting dinner when that voice in my mind said, "Check the auditorium." I argued with it, assuring myself there was no need. I had a receipt for the rental in my desk. A few minutes later the voice came again, with greater urgency. Again I put myself through a mental argument, scolding myself for being so nervous about the speaker, and put the voice out of my mind. A third time the message came. This time I seemed to feel an annoyance with me for ignoring "them" or "it," and a sense of real urgency.

Feeling a bit foolish, I called the school. Just to make it sound as if I had a good reason for calling, I asked the secretary if the custodian knew how we wanted the table and chairs set up in the lobby. Her reply astounded me. She asked me what I was talking about. There was nothing on the calendar for use of the auditorium that evening. I very quickly explained that we had rented it and I had a receipt. She was not impressed, and told me that only the head office of the school district could do anything about it. I called them; they too had no record of our transaction. However, since the auditorium was free that evening we could use it if I would come down and fill out the proper forms.

I had to rush to get to the office before closing time. As I was filling out the new forms the secretary approached me apologetically and showed me the original application. It had been misfiled.

They barely had time to call the custodian before he left and instruct him to be there to open the school for us.

I have often thought of that experience. If two hundred people and a speaker had arrived to find a closed and locked auditorium, it would have been most embarrassing for us. As far as I knew, none of us would have known how to reach anyone who could have let us in. My "voice" had indeed saved us from a minor catastrophe. But "who" or "what" knew that our reservation was not on the school calendar, and that we would be locked out?

Two well-publicized individuals, both born in England, possess skills attributed to contact with intelligent, talented, and famous-in-their-time spirits. Their experiences have been well-documented, and I include them here because their authenticity cannot be questioned. An explanation of their contributions in the field of music and art is, as always, a matter of individual preference.

The Case of Rosemary Brown

One morning when she was seven, lying in bed waiting to be called by her mother, Rosemary Brown felt a presence. Turning about, she found herself facing a man with long hair, dressed in unfamiliar period clothing. Although she was frightened, his first words were reassuring. He told her that she had a special destiny, and that when she was older he would come to her again and they would work together. Then he disappeared. She forgot about this visitation for some time until, one day while she was studying, she turned a page in her high school textbook and found herself staring in amazement at a photograph of the man she had seen in her bedroom. The name under the photograph identified the man as Franz Liszt, Hungarian composer and pianist. She pondered this for some time. What did it mean? More years passed. She married, then was widowed. Once again she was confronted by the apparition of Liszt, who now explained that she was to write music, and that he would help her.

Thus began a new life for her in music, although she knew very little about the field. She had had only a few piano lessons in her entire life. Before long Liszt introduced her to other famous composers: Beethoven, Chopin, Debussy, Schumann, Bach, Rachmaninoff, and Schubert. Liszt was very kind and thoughtful of her feelings. He personally introduced her to the other composers, remaining with her until she felt comfortable working with them. He frequently gave her advice on personal problems in her life.

Liszt explained to her that these personalities were not using her to compose new music just to give the world more music. They intended to prove that they were not dead, and that their talents could be shared through people like her.

Eventually her compositions came to the attention of the music world in her country. England may be known for its haunted castles and monasteries, but the musical establishment was not ready to buy Mrs. Brown's story regarding the source of her talents. However, the compositions were of such high quality that musicians were intrigued. Some who tested her insisted that, given her slim musical education and limited skills as a pianist, she could not possibly have been the composer of the works they examined. On one occasion when Leonard Bernstein was in London, he invited Rosemary to be his dinner guest. She was instructed by Rachmaninoff's spirit to take certain pieces of music with her, which she did. Bernstein was highly impressed.

Then one of the major studios offered her a challenge. She was to write a new composition on the air in the presence of a number of recognized musicians. Although she was frightened, Liszt assured her that she must do it. He promised that she would have the help that was always available to her when she sat to compose. At the studio, as she began to write the music, she was given one time signature for the treble clef and a different one for the bass clef. In addition, the notes seemed so complicated they did not make sense to her. Her fears increased to the point that she could scarcely keep her composure. Liszt continued to assure her that all was going well.

When she had completed the composition, she was unable to play it. In fact, only one pianist in the group had the skills to perform her composition on the piano. All were amazed at its beauty and complexity. She had passed the test. Her music was sold in France and then in America on discs and as sheet music.

Musicians who studied her works were highly impressed by the similarity of the music she composed to the known works of the composers she claimed were helping her. Her complete story is told in her biography, *Unfinished Symphonies*, published in 1971 by William Morrow and Co. Inc., New York. It makes fascinating reading. Sir George Trevelyan said of her, "I am convinced that these beings use Rosemary Brown to prove that there is an existence after death. In this materialistic world, this will free large numbers of people from doubt and fear..." Hephzibah Menuhin wrote, "There is no question that she is a very sincere woman. The music is absolutely in the style of these composers." The composer Rodney Bennett said of her, "I was having trouble with a piece of music and she passed along Debussy's recommendation — which worked ... A lot of people can improvise but you couldn't fake music like this without years of training."[18]

The music produced by Rosemary Brown provides evidence, difficult to refute, that musicians of a past era are communicating their presence and their skills through a living person.

Matthew Manning's Art

Matthew Manning has been called the most gifted psychic in our century by numerous researchers and investigators. A research center in Canada invited him to visit their laboratory for special testing. They claim to be the first to measure the brain waves of psychics while they are receiving information from some extra-worldly source. During their examination, his alpha waves went into violent spasms of activity, showing on the graph the largest swings of anything they had ever measured. Matthew was so annoyed by the repeated tests, and by the attitude of the many researchers who treated him as if he were some kind of a fraud, that he finally refused to be an experimental subject. He is currently living in England and is the director of a healing center. He lectures and sees private clients.

Matthew was born in England. When he was approximately nine years old, strange things began to happen in his house. Furniture would be totally rearranged. The family would straighten it, leave the room, and return minutes later to find everything topsy-turvy again, as his mother described it. Nothing was ever broken or damaged, and no noise accompanied these events. Since no one was ever hurt, the family simply lived with this strange phenomenon, until it was time for Matthew to go to private school. At that point his father became concerned that he would suffer ridicule from his classmates if the phenomena occurred in school.

He made an appointment with the headmaster of the school and frankly told him of the poltergeist activity. The headmaster made light of it. He assured the father that boys' schools were notorious for juvenile pranks; he was certain he could handle the situation. However, it was not long after Matthew began school that strange things happened in the dormitory. Silverware would fly through the air, heavy bunk beds were moved about, and doors were held shut. At first, the boys were frightened. Soon, however, they learned to pay little attention to the disturbances, since the flying objects always missed the students and no one was ever hurt. One incident amused everyone. The one boy who was really frightened took a Bible to bed with him, and the activity around him increased to an intensity much greater than in any other place in the dorm.

One day while Matthew was studying, his hand seemed to be taken over by an unseen force. Writing was produced on his paper without his conscious volition. It was then that he discovered that when he did automatic writing, the poltergeist activity ceased. For a school history project he needed some information, but he could not find it because the books he required had been damaged in a flood. He was told not to worry, but to go ahead and work on the project. "They" would give him the information he needed.

When he went into his room he discovered that a number of dated signatures had been written on the walls of his bedroom. They were the names of the men he wanted for his project. Each time he used the names and dates given to him, he would return to his room and find more names. Finally even the ceiling was covered with signatures. All of them were unique. Furthermore, when compared with signatures taken from the individuals' writing when they had been alive, the signatures were accurate reproductions.

In addition to the many strange experiences to which Matthew was subjected, he was given information about many things that could be and were checked out and proven to be accurate. Among his many psychic gifts was spoonbending. He once said that he wanted to do something useful with his life, and he could not think of anything more banal than continually bending spoons.

One day his hand was directed to drawing. Soon he was producing all kinds of pictures, from people to animals, with tremendous speed. A number of famous painters supposedly expressed themselves through him. He was informed of their identity. The pictures that appeared under his hand began with a few simple strokes; often he had no idea what the finished product would be. If it was a face, the first stroke might be a beard, or a nose, or an eye. Eventually the rest of the picture would be filled out. The artists working through him were frequently identified by their styles. The portraits attributed to Durer, the famous German engraver, were most notable in their similarity to works produced during Durer's lifetime. Some of the artists could not be identified; many of Matthew's beautiful bird pictures were not claimed by any known artists. He was very aware of the personalities who drew through his hands and was uncomfortable when Picasso worked with him. Matthew said Picasso had a violent temper. At times, if not pleased with the results, Picasso would throw the pen or jab it into the paper.

Matthew was very serious about his gift and his destiny. He believed he was here to help people, so his days of demonstrating spectacular phenomena came to an end. If anyone has proven the reality of communication between the physical and spiritual worlds, he has. His life since then has been dedicated to helping people. He lectures, teaches, counsels, and is a very powerful healer.

I first heard of Matthew when I attended a Psychotronics Congress in Monte Carlo. A film shown at the Congress so impressed many of us that I bought a copy, and have shared it with interested schools and organizations. It is certainly one of the finest, most well-documented films on psychic phenomena that I have seen. When I met Matthew he told me that another, later film is even better. A book about Matthew, entitled *The Link*, was published in the United States in 1975 by Holt, Rinehart and Winston, New York. It is fascinating reading for anyone interested in a *bona fide* account of a highly gifted sensitive.

In the next chapter I would like to introduce and briefly discuss a totally different kind of haunting. I call it pseudo-haunting because no intelligent entities seem to be involved in the demonstrations.

---

1. Lawrence Tunstall Heron, *ESP in the Bible* (Garden City, NY: Doubleday & Co., Inc., 1970), 48.
2. Frances Vaughn, *Awakening Intuition* (Anchor Books, 1979), 145.
3. Willis Harman and Howard Rheingold, *Higher Creativity* (Los Angeles: Jeremy P. Tarcher, Inc., 1984), 31.
4. *Fate*, December 1981.
5. Harman and Rheingold, 20, 42.
6. Ibid., 30.
7. Ibid., 46.
8. Ibid., 45–47.
9. Ibid., 35.
10. Ibid., 75–77.
11. Ibid., 54–55.
12. Ibid., 41.
13. Ibid., 46.
14. Ibid., 23.
15. Ibid., 45.
16. Heron, 44–45.
17. Joseph Millard, *Edgar Cayce: Mystery Man of Miracles* (Greenwich, CT: Fawcett Gold Medal Books, 1967).
18. From the album notes to *Musical Seance*, a Warner Brothers recording featuring Rosemary Brown, accompanied by Peter Catin, piano.

CHAPTER 13

Pseudo-Hauntings

The Case of Abraham Lincoln

When one reads that the spirit of Abraham Lincoln still haunts the White House, and many who live there have substantiated such a claim, one is prone to wonder if such a great man has nothing better to do than remain in his former environment. Why, with his intellectual prowess, has he not moved into other dimensions of activity and continued to work for the emancipation of all human beings?

A body of interesting statistics indicates that he has indeed projected his energy into our own time to work for a better world. The following information will be classified by many as no more than coincidence. For those who sense order and purpose in all events and in individual lives, the parallels between the lives of Lincoln and John F. Kennedy indicate a soul connection that could be a continuous expression of a soul whose destiny was to emancipate the oppressed.

Lincoln was elected president in 1860, Kennedy in 1960. Both were slain on a Friday in the presence of their wives. Both were shot in the head, from behind. Their successors, both named Johnson, were Southern Democrats, and had been in the senate. Andrew Johnson was born in 1808; Lyndon Johnson in 1908.

John Wilkes Booth was born in 1839; Lee Harvey Oswald in 1939. Booth and Oswald, both southerners, favored unpopular ideas. Both presidents lost children through death while in the White House. Lincoln's secretary, named Kennedy, advised him

127

not to go to the theater. Kennedy's secretary, named Lincoln, advised him not to go to Dallas. John Wilkes Booth shot Lincoln in a theater and ran to a warehouse. Lee Harvey Oswald shot Kennedy from a warehouse and ran to a theater. The names "Kennedy" and "Lincoln" each contain seven letters. The names "Andrew Johnson" and "Lyndon Johnson" each contain thirteen letters. The names "John Wilkes Booth" and "Lee Harvey Oswald" each contain fifteen letters. Both assassins were killed before being brought to trial. Both Johnsons were opposed for reelection by men whose names started with "G."

Documents now available confirm that Lincoln and Mrs. Lincoln held at least five seances in the White House. Although Lincoln was skeptical of metaphysics, his attitude changed when certain predictions concerning the Civil War proved to be accurate. An astrologer predicted Lincoln's assassination.

Three days before the assassination Lincoln had a vision of walking into the stateroom and seeing a casket lying in state. When he asked the attendants who had died they wept and told him the president had been killed.

So much for the paranormal events that provide a background for the belief that Lincoln still haunts the White House. Many guests there have reported seeing a "ghost" emerge from a certain bedroom into the hall. One photograph taken of Mrs. Lincoln and Todd after Lincoln's death includes a clear image of Mr. Lincoln in the background. The remarkable thing about the image is that he was dressed in a suit that had never been photographed in his lifetime. The image could not have been somehow dubbed into the photograph of his wife and son. This practice, unfortunately, is not uncommon among developers who wish to fake spirit pictures.

Some answers to these questions can be found by again examining the nature of energy. Pure energy is formless, impersonal; it has no individualized intelligence. It has shape and form only when intelligent energy creates that shape and form. An energy form created by traumatic events seems to be charged with a powerful energy that continues to exist, in the form created, for a considerable length of time. Supposedly it will eventually dissipate. While it still has form it continually repeats a pattern commensurate with its original experience. In the case of a haunting, the form is seen to repeat patterns of behavior such as walking up or down stairs, going in and out of a specific door, appearing over a mantel, or pacing a hallway.

Manifestations of this kind can be seen clearly by highly sensitive clairvoyants. They are also often seen by people who are unaware of their psychic ability. For them, such encounters can be a terrifying experience. A clairvoyant knows the difference between a discarnate presence and an energy form: the latter cannot communicate. However, a good clairvoyant can generally pick up the major details of the event that created the energy form. This will be illustrated in a case history later in this chapter.

Presumably the reason that these forms are created and remain so long on the earth plane is that they were caused by a very traumatic event. The mind of the person or persons involved suffered great mental and/or emotional shock and pain. This generates the energy form, which remains after the individual who created it has departed, usually in death.

In order to give you a better understanding of energy as it manifests in response to mental activity, I will present three related examples. The first is the concept of thought forms. C. W. Leadbeater has written an excellent little volume, with color illustrations, in which he describes the energies that emanate from the mind as a result of the thinking process. The pictures are representations of the images clairvoyants see above or around the head of the individual under observation. Thoughts of rage produce sharp shafts of muddy red which dart out from the body. Thoughts of greed also appear in dark red, but this form has curved appendages resembling claws or hooks. Spiritual thoughts produce shades of lavender and blue, and appear in beautiful shapes and designs. Sadness and depression appear as gray and black shades. If the thoughts are clear and purposefully motivated the form is well-defined. Scattered or nebulous thoughts produce a vague form, like a splash of color. Sensitive people are often affected by the energy of these thought forms. Since the forms are often created out of traumatic events, their energy is negative and destructive.

Trapped Energy

Without a doubt the most baffling case Freda and I ever faced occurred on a huge, beautiful estate set on a hill, surrounded by an acre or so of elegantly landscaped grounds. Mrs. Freeland was alone when we arrived at her door. She invited us in and, explaining that her story was a long one, suggested that we make ourselves comfortable in her sunroom, which faced the garden.

129

The house had been built by a wealthy engineer. Although he raised his family in the house, the engineer was apparently a very unhappy man. He was estranged from his three children, who claimed to hate him, and he had been married three times. He had a reputation in the community for being a ladies' man. At one point he tried to commit suicide by shooting himself. This attempt failed, leaving him physically handicapped. Eventually he succeeded in killing himself with poison rather than a gun.

Three families had lived in the house since the engineer's death, and disaster had struck each of them. In the first family the man strangled his wife in the upstairs bedroom. The husband had been convicted and was serving time. In the second family there was another suicide; Mrs. Freeland thought the victim was a son. The third family suffered numerous problems with a grown son, who wrecked his car three times during their residence in the house.

In all three instances, according to Mrs. Freeland, the families had been well-adjusted and functional until they moved into this house. The pattern of disaster seemed to consist of problems affecting only the male members of the families. After these men moved into the house their personalities seemed to change. They became belligerent, quarrelsome, irritable, and accident-prone.

We asked Mrs. Freeland why she would take a chance on a house with such a reputation. She said the price was so attractive she could not pass it up, since she really liked the property. She emphasized that she was not superstitious and believed she was in no danger. She had a grown son and daughter. The son was in his late teens and lived at home. The daughter was married and lived in another town.

She said that soon after they moved into the house her son started having problems. He wrecked his car twice, and barely escaped being seriously hurt. These incidents reminded her of the past history of the house. As it became increasingly difficult to live with her son, she began to wonder if there might be something to the "curse," as she termed it. That was when she called us. They had been living in the house for approximately a year and a half. She said she had thought it was her imagination, but she felt uncomfortable in certain spots in the house: at the foot of the main stairway, and in one of the upstairs bedrooms.

She had learned that the engineer had shot himself at the foot of the stairs. The upstairs bedroom was supposedly the room in which he had murdered his wife.

It was now time for us to explore the house. Sometimes I accompanied Freda in her exploration, an appropriate step on this occasion because Mrs. Freeland was giving us a guided tour. I had never been physically or emotionally aware of spirits or energies up until this visit, but when we walked into that upstairs bedroom I felt goose bumps spring up on my arms. The atmosphere was heavily oppressive; I wanted out. Freda, of course, was also aware of the energy, but immediately stated that no spirit was present, only the negative charges left from the murder.

As we traversed the balance of the house she was certain that no spirit entities were present, only the powerful energies of rage and resentment created by the traumatic events of the past. As we entered the kitchen, a bright, sunny room, Freda was surprised to discover only positive light energy there, with no hint of negativity. Mrs. Freeland was impressed. She said that the kitchen had been added, to her specifications, at the time she bought the house. It was the only room in which she felt comfortable; since it was large and faced part of the garden, she spent most of her time there.

Although Freda had never dealt with a house haunted only by negative energies, her inner guidance assured her she could dispel them. Over a period of two weeks she visited the house every three days. She meditated to fill the house with white light, which would displace the dark energies. Whatever the explanation, it worked. Mrs. Freeland was very grateful. She assured us that negative energy no longer hung heavy in her house. In a later follow-up she reported that her son's disposition had undergone a remarkable turn-around; he was his old, pleasant self again.

It was interesting that Freda was inspired to dissipate the negative energy using white light, rather than by meditating on dispelling the dark energy. It could be analogous to physical light and dark. When light is turned on, darkness no longer exists.

A Perpetual Duel

Another interesting case reported in the literature concerns an old house in Philadelphia. More than one psychic invited to visit this house has seen a duel being fought on the stairs.

The sounds of conflict supposedly have been heard by inhabitants of the house, always at the same time of day. The sound resembles the clashing of swords, accompanied by some thumps, as if someone was jumping about. These sounds have been report-ed by numerous people who have been in the house.

Investigators invited psychics to visit the house to see if they could come up with an explanation. They reported that, although they could not communicate with the perpetrators of the noise, they saw two men with swords fighting on the stair, moving up and down as they fought. They concluded that these were simply energy forms trapped in a continually repeating pattern.

The second half of *True Hauntings* addresses a different aspect of spirit phenomena — the question of possession, invasion, overlap-ping, or psychic attack. Whatever one wishes to call it, it is the intrusion of spirit entities into the daily lives of human beings.

A chapter on mediumship, now called channeling, has been included because of this practice's current popularity and potential destructive energy.

CHAPTER 14

Personal Invasions

What is Psychic Attack?

The alarmingly common phenomenon of psychic attack is terribly frightening to many people. Almost everyone is subject to psychic attack, and few of us escape some form of it. If you have an enemy who frequently sends resentful thoughts in your direction, you are the object of a psychic attack. If you have a parent who dominates you through mind power, you are suffering a form of control. You have been victimized, even if your parent has never abused you physically.

A young lady in one of my classes came to me one evening and said, "I can make my mother say what I want her to say. I can ask permission to go someplace and make her say 'yes.' Sometimes she wants to change her mind, and I just laugh and remind her that she has already said 'yes.' Can you teach me how to make my roommate do what I want her to do?" Needless to say I gave that young lady a lesson on why we have no right to try to control another human being. I am not at all sure she heard me. This particular phenomenon has been recognized, feared, ignored, written about, vigorously refuted, and exploited for centuries. Endless volumes have dealt with it in both profane and religious history. There is probably no culture through the centuries of recorded history that has not recognized its influence on human lives and dealt with it in conformance with its own set of moral and religious values.

Two Major Forces

According to the literature there are two major forces invading and interfering in humanity's domain. The most common force, the one with which I am most familiar, purportedly originates in the realm of the physically dead, often referred to as the spirit world. In this dimension the degrees of activity are legion, manifesting as everything from the most gentle of invaders to vicious intruders intent upon revenge.

The second major force is considered to be demonic. This force belongs to a totally different body of created beings who have never been in human form. Their major purpose is to harass and destroy all who respond to their energy. They talk incessantly but their conversation is limited to information that is in the victim's memory, and they lack the ability to reason in abstractions.

These observations come from Dr. Wilson Van Dusen's seventeen years' experience in an institution working with the mentally ill. He performed extensive research, exploring as faithfully as possible the hallucinations of his patients. Some years later he discovered that the experiences of his patients followed the pattern of Emanuel Swedenborg's unusual doctrines regarding the mentally ill. Although Swedenborg wrote in the eighteenth century, his findings so impressed Dr. Van Dusen that he made an in-depth study of them. In doing so, he found answers for some of the puzzling aspects of the hallucinations experienced by his own patients.[1]

A basic tenet of Swedenborg's philosophy was that a person's life depends on his or her relationship with a hierarchy of spirits. Dr. Van Dusen found that his patients consistently believed that they were in contact with an order of beings in another world. In recent years a number of psychologists have been investigating the possible connection between mental illness and spirit possession. When Lotte Von Strahl, a world-famous psychic, came to Los Angeles, she worked with a psychiatrist who wished to remain anonymous. Together they sought to identify patients who were actually mentally ill, in contrast to those who were possessed and responding to their tormentors.

According to the findings of Dr. Van Dusen, members of the lower order of psychic forces were persistent in undermining the patients, screaming into their minds, and reacting violently to any mention of religion. They sought to destroy their victim's conscience and worked against all higher values. They were capable of impersonation, deception, and outright lies. Apparently they were not capable of abstract thought or sequential reasoning. Although these characteristics were noted in mentally ill patients, they do not necessarily apply to individuals outside of mental institutions who are possessed.

Multiple Personalities

Aberrant behavior provides psychologists with a fertile field in which to investigate psychic invasion. In addition to those mental illnesses which require institutional confinement, multiple-personality or split-personality disorders can be found in members of the general populace. These individuals may function in one personality for a number of hours or days, then take on a totally different personality at an undetermined future time. Some people may assume three, four, or more personalities over a period of time. These personalities often have no recollection of each other. The person may have no awareness of the behavior of any personality except the one they currently occupy. There are numerous explanations for this phenomena, and many psychologists have spent considerable time and effort in treating these people in the hopes of returning them to one stable personality. However, a considerable number of therapists believe that the accurate diagnosis for this condition is possession by a spirit entity.

Evidence of the need for professionals to assist people who have unpleasant encounters with the spirit world can be found in all cultures. In England the Reverend Canon John D. Pearce-Higgins, formerly vice-provost of Southwark Cathedral, received requests for help from approximately three thousand people in 1971–72. Of these, 540 requests were for psychic help in hauntings or possession.

Witchcraft

Through a long period of human history, possession and hysterical manifestations attributed to possession were believed to be the result of spells cast by witches. Many thousands of innocent people were imprisoned and burned because of the superstitions of the masses. Unscrupulous individuals preyed on the fears and ignorance of the people, a fact that is well-illustrated by John Darrell, the notorious exorcist whose dubious practices prompted the Church of England to outlaw exorcism in 1603. Only a few years later, in 1692, the witch trials in Salem made history with hundreds arrested and nineteen victims hanged.

Witchcraft has for centuries carried the stigma of evil. The dictionary states that one meaning of the word "witch" is "a woman supposedly under the influence of evil spirits, who possesses magic powers." The word comes from the old Anglo-Saxon *wicca*, which means "wise one"; therefore witchcraft is a craft of the wise. At the present time many witches, particularly in England, claim that their special gifts, primarily of healing, are used for the good of humanity, never for evil. In many cultures the witch-doctor is a highly respected member of the tribe who works with the laws of nature for the good of tribal members.

The Source of Power

A primary question to consider is the source of a person's power. Power users in different societies use a wide variety of names: witches, warlocks, medicine men, satanists, wizards. Many such power users purportedly get their powers from beings in another dimension. Unfortunately, the general consensus in some cultures is that those beings are evil and take control of their "followers" in exchange for the favors they grant. Are we to surmise, then, that all who possess special powers beyond the capacities of the average human being are controlled by discarnate entities, whether good or evil?

This is indeed a sobering thought. Spiritual healers, whose powers cannot be disputed, exist in every community on the globe. All claim that the power comes THROUGH them, not from them. Olga Worrall, one of the most famous healers of our century, worked with her husband in Baltimore for twenty-five years, healing people from all over the world. Researchers thoroughly investigated her healing abilities. Instruments measured the energy emanating from her hands as she used them for healing. She used her powers to affect the growth of plants under rigid test conditions. What is the source of such powers? People who possess this healing ability say they cannot control their compulsion to use it. If they are near an ill person, their hands get hot and they feel they must place them on the suffering individual. Is someone possessing them during that act?

Obviously the origin of the control must be examined. What is its purpose? Observation indicates that the powers manifesting in our world range from those intending evil and harassment, up to those offering the highest forms of loving support and assistance. At what stage, then, do we label an intervention in our lives by spirit forces a state of possession or invasion? When is it expedient to call for assistance from an individual skilled in what is now termed "spirit releasement?"

Continuum Hypothesis

Perhaps the whole matter can be better understood by postulating a continuum in the spiritual dimension. At the very bottom of the continuum are the evil spirit energies, which for greater clarity in this description we will call demons or daemons (although in some disciplines the latter are classified simply as supernatural beings, not necessarily evil).

Going up the scale of the continuum we encounter the spirits who have at one time manifested in a physical form. Here begins the innumerable gradations of spiritual understanding. The first spirits above the demons are ignorant, angry, resentful, and vindictive. They harass any human being whose energy is low and coincides with their own negative attitudes. At the next level are those whose deaths left them bewildered, frightened, lost, and seeking help of some kind. They will often attach themselves to someone whose aura is strong, probably a sensitive individual. The spirits hope this person can help them, or at least provide a safe place for them to stay.

Next we move up to the many spirits who left the earth plane with unfinished business. They frequently attach themselves to someone who is responsive to their thoughts. They impel their host to undertake activities to satisfy their own desires, which may range from getting drunk to supporting some philanthropic cause.

Ouija board-pushers and table-tippers occupy the next level. Again, these spirits differ widely in their purpose. Many are responding to the invitation of the owners of these objects. These are ignorant energies who enjoy playing games with gullible people. Their information is seldom accurate and their advice is often detrimental. I have had numerous clients who were emotionally disturbed after playing with friends around a ouija board. The spirit, having been invited to communicate with people, decides to stay and reside in its host.

Another category of spirits consists of good energies who are not highly advanced, but who sincerely want to help humanity. Some of these have been described earlier; see chapter 3, "The Case of Alicia," for an example. Spirits from this group will often respond positively to ouija board-sitters; their information may be helpful and fairly accurate. Since their motive is to be helpful, they would never attempt to possess a physical person, but they certainly manifest enough power to affect the lives of human beings.

On a much higher level, certainly, are the spirits who left their physical bodies after having lived long, useful, productive lives – scientists, doctors, humanitarians. The evidence suggests that they want to share their expertise and knowledge with humanity. Their communications are reliable, accurate, and most often conveyed to human beings through mental impressions. However, some information comes through dreams and psychic insights. Some years ago, *Osteopathic* magazine devoted an entire issue to parapsychology. The central theme of the articles presented was that consistently successful business executives followed their hunches, regardless of the advice of their colleagues.

So a very major question is, where do hunches come from? Many people believe they have a guardian angel, and that this Spirit Being guides their lives through mind or mental telepathy. This type of communication also has varying degrees of expression. Individuals often admit that they have no idea why they made certain decisions; they felt they HAD to. Others speak of hearing a voice in their minds, as if someone was putting the idea into their heads. Some get the message in visions; others have only a "feeling." Since this is obviously control from something outside of the individual, is it a psychic attack, even though the motive may be for good?

In any event, this type of communication is almost certainly advantageous to humanity. Therefore at some point on our continuum invasion ceases to be destructive, because it apparently originates from a more highly evolved spirit energy.

Channeling

Where does channeling fit into this model? Does it differ in any significant way from mediumship? Channeling, now the accepted term for spirit communication, has become a popular subject. Technically, the term covers any method that purports to receive information from any dimension beyond the known physical world. Channeling also follows the continuum hypothesis. Because of this, much of present-day channeling is unreliable and downright dangerous. On the other hand, gifted artists, writers, healers, and inventors seem to be channeling highly advanced and knowledgeable spiritual beings.

While most of these communications, according to the recipients, are mental or telepathic in nature, there are exceptions. George Washington at Valley Forge "saw" his communicator. The being spoke to him in a thunderous voice, giving him information about the development of the Republic and predicting major events for the future, including the great wars. Dr. Elizabeth Kubler Ross was visited by a woman who had been dead for six months. The visitation was so real she demanded that the visitor sign a paper so she would have evidence. This experience changed Dr. Ross's whole life and literally pushed her into the wonderful work she has done in the field of death and dying.

I have had numerous clients who saw their communicator. Sometimes the figure was as solid as a physical person; at other times the apparition was transparent. The visitor might appear only partially, perhaps just the upper torso and head, or consist of a vision of a total individual. These experiences, reported by sane and normal individuals, are too common to be classified as mental illness or hallucinations.

Are the imaginary playmates of small children, reported in all cultures, spirit visitors? With their minds not yet indoctrinated by the limits of the physical world, are children actually in touch with the spiritual dimension? Their stories and experiences are legion. Many of the reports come from individuals who have later become famous in all professions and disciplines of modern life. Often they credit their experiences with their imaginary playmates as having a strong influence on their lives, their choice of vocations, professions, and behavior.

Summary

The focus of this chapter has been to determine what a psychic attack is and does. Perhaps the general statement can be made that human beings normally have a relationship with a spiritual dimension. However, there are many degrees or levels of awareness in the physical dimension as well as in the spiritual dimension. We attract or communicate with the spirit energies that are most compatible with our own, whether we are aware of this phenomenon or not. At this stage of our development as humans, we are for the most part insensitive to the spiritual energies around us. This does not mean we do not interrelate constantly; we simply are not aware of this relationship.

Unconscious communication becomes hazardous and disruptive to the personality only when it is destructive in its manifestation. This occurs when the invading spirit is bent on its own self-centered expression, or selects a victim with vengeful intent. In such cases, a therapist skillful in communicating with discarnates can assist in removing the offending energy and sending it to "The Light."

The following chapters present case histories in which, for the most part, the invading energies have been responsible for creating disruptive experiences in individuals. A special chapter on channeling has been included to include positive aspects of communication. The final chapter addresses the overall benefits that humanity can experience by developing a sensitivity to the spiritual dimension.

---

1. Emanuel Swedenborg, *Heaven and Hell* (London: Swedenborg Society, 1937).

CHAPTER 15

A Three-Century Vendetta

A very dear and valued friend confided to me that she often lost her temper. Since I had never seen any manifestation of this in all the years we had worked together, it was hard for me to believe. I had seen her handle the most trying situations with a smile and composure that I considered quite remarkable. Nothing ever seemed to upset her cheerful disposition. In a crisis she could always be depended upon to come up with a solution, and her genuine concern for the welfare and comfort of her friends and co-workers was apparent in all of her relationships.

The violent outbursts which she described to me occurred almost entirely within her family, particularly between her and her husband. She admitted that she often realized she was being unreasonable, and that the events did not justify the rage she felt. The idea of spirit invasion seemed so out of character for this beautiful lady, beloved by everyone, that I was very hesitant to even suggest such a diagnosis of her problem.

However, as we discussed her growing concern, I asked if she would be offended if I tested her for possession. To my surprise she was quite willing. She had thought of that possibility herself, since she felt so helpless when these rages came over her.

She was an excellent hypnotic subject, and in a matter of seconds was in an altered state. When I asked if someone was with her who would be willing to talk with me, her voice changed slightly and the answer came: "Yes, I am with her all the time and I am not going to leave."

Although this spirit was quite willing to talk about himself and his reason for staying with her, he stated very clearly that he had no intention of leaving her. I had the feeling that he was afraid of where he would go if he left, although he did not specifically voice that fear.

I began questioning him. He was quite responsive, answering my questions without hesitation.

"Why are you using her body this way? Who are you?"

"My name doesn't matter now, but it was Pierre. I was an architect in France."

"Why do you make her angry sometimes?"

"Because I am angry."

"But why take it out on her?"

"Because she was once one of my judges."

"How long ago was that?"

"It was in 1692."

"Are you telling me you have been with this person all that time, since 1692?"

"No. Some of the time I got into others who were my judges."

"But why? What did they do that would make you spend all these years trapped in physical bodies when you could be a free soul in your dimension?"

"What they did was not fair. I want to make them suffer as they made me suffer."

"I would like to hear about what happened to you. Can you tell me what they did to you?"

Pierre related the details of his experience in France in 1692. As a successful architect he had been commissioned by the city to design a bridge. His design was accepted and built. However, it later collapsed. Pierre was blamed for the tragedy, which killed a number of people. All of his efforts to convince his accusers that the fault lay with the contractors, who had used inferior material, were of no avail. He was tried by a jury, found guilty, and executed in a most disgraceful way. He was hanged, and then his head was placed on a hook in the public square for all to see and spit at. It was left there until the birds plucked out his eyes and fed on his flesh. This, he explained, was the most disgraceful and humiliating treatment that could be meted out to criminals. His family suffered disgrace because of his sentence, and his own good name and reputation were forever sullied. He was helpless to change this outrageous sentence and treatment, and he was innocent.

His rage knew no bounds. He vowed to get even with all of the members of that jury. Over the intervening years he spent time with each one of them, moving from one to the other and making their lives difficult in different ways. He had trouble controlling my friend because she was such a good person. However, she and her husband had the usual family problems as they struggled with finances and the raising of five children. About the only power he had over her was to increase her anger when she became frustrated.

I finally said to him, "You were an educated man, a man of the upper class. Surely you must be tired of following people around just to harass them. And think for a minute. These personalities are totally different people from the ones who condemned you. Maybe they are the same souls, but they are certainly not the same people. They are totally unaware of having hurt you. Aren't you tired of behaving this way?"

His voice sounded tired and unhappy as he responded, "Yes, it does get very boring. I am not enjoying it any more. But where can I go, what can I do?"

I asked him if he could think of someone in his dimension whom he had loved, or who had loved him — perhaps his mother.

He replied that he had so disgraced his family they would not want to have anything to do with him. He also said that he had really loved his mother, and she loved him and had been proud of him.

I explained that there were souls in his dimension who would help him if he asked for help, but that he had to ask and really want to change. I told him about the light into which he could move to become free of his entrapment in the earth plane.

As I was talking he interrupted me. His voice, through my friend of course, sounded happy. He said, "My mother has just come in. She is taking my hand. She says, 'Son, I am so happy. Now we can be together again.'" Pierre went on to tell me that she explained to him that she could take him to a place where he could be happy. So he had decided to go with her. He thanked me for helping him to be free and expressed relief that he could let go of his ugly past.

My friend's voice changed back to its normal pitch. She expressed a feeling of freedom, as if a weight had been lifted from her. She was surprised at the story that had unfolded for her, but stated that it felt right and that she could accept it.

Why had Pierre's mother not come to help him sooner? Did this indicate that she was still in the spirit world? I do not know, and I confess to being skeptical during such experiences. It is difficult for me to accept that intelligent energies, which I cannot see or feel, are actually interacting in my presence. I only know that something important is happening to my clients. It is very real to them, real enough that changes take place in their lives and problems, often of long standing, are resolved.

In this particular case, the arrival of Pierre's mother is consistent with metaphysical teachings. She could not reach him as long as he maintained resentment and a desire for revenge. As soon as he let go and desired to be free, she was able to communicate with him. There is plenty of evidence that spirits remain in the disembodied state for a long period of time. If the tie had been strong between them, she might have been waiting for just such a time when he would give up his rage and they could be reunited.

If such experiences were rare they might justifiably be classified as hallucinations or imaginative creations. However, the prevalence of such experiences in therapy demands a more valid explanation or diagnosis. Many of these people have had no prior experience with altered states of consciousness, nor any background in metaphysics. Therefore they are not, even subconsciously, reacting to some preconceived idea gleaned from reading or hearsay. For many clients the entire subject of metaphysics, psychics, spirits, and paranormal communication is entirely new. They approach the idea with considerable skepticism. Yet their experience may include purported contact with entities in another dimension, and they are unable to refute the information that comes in this way.

On the other hand, if all knowledge is in some sort of a universal "mind bank," is it possible that human beings have the ability to tune in to any information of any kind, even to the extent of being selective? Simply by "thought" are we able to attract scenarios that describe and/or explain any situation at any particular moment in time? Such clairvoyant ability could explain many paranormal events that heretofore have been given other explanations. Granted that the mind may have these capacities, it still does not adequately explain many of the mystical experiences common to all cultures.

At this point in time we possess many explanations and a wealth of data about the paranormal, as well as consistent patterns of experiences that seem to conform to certain metaphysical principles. If we are ever to know the truth about the powers of our minds and the relationship of our physical world to the non-physical dimension, it behooves us to keep an open mind and to critically examine all paranormal phenomena with an unbiased approach.

In the next chapter we will explore a case in which the culture of the subject demanded vengeance, but the soul rejected such behavior and required penance and recognition of spiritual law. Through a long series of events in the current life, the young man finally found peace of mind through age regression and spirit releasement.

CHAPTER 16

The Egyptian Murders

The phone rang persistently at 11:00 P.M. When I answered, the voice on the other end sounded frightened and distraught. I had known the young lady, Kathy, for a number of years in a social way, and her husband Clarence since his teen years. "Please come right away. My husband is in one of his rages. I know he is not crazy, but if I call the police they will lock him up."

Through her conversation I could hear her husband's voice. It sounded more like the roar of a lion than the yells of a human being. She told me that he was not responsive to her efforts to calm him. He had ripped out one of the pillars in their room divider as he stormed through the house, roaring obscenities.

I called Freda. She had gone to bed, but she dressed hurriedly while I drove to her house to pick her up. I had no intention of attempting to handle the situation without her psychic expertise to guide us. As we drove to Clarence and Kathy's home, Freda tuned in to the problem. She told me it was a very long and involved case. Clarence would need counseling to rid himself of the entity that had been with him since he was a five-year-old boy.

When we arrived at the house we found the three children hovering in the background, a little subdued but apparently not frightened. Kathy assured us that their father had never harmed any of them when he was in these "spells." She took us to the bedroom. Clarence was lying on the bed, his arms flung out wide and his legs spread apart. His eyes were closed, but when we entered he opened them and, with a loud roar, raised his body to a sitting position. His eyes glared at us with a vacant sort of stare, as if he was not focusing on us.

We approached the bed. Freda went to one side and I to the other, and we each took one of his arms and gently pressed him back on the bed. He was a large, strong man and we knew he could have knocked us both to the floor, but he passively relaxed under our pressure as Freda talked to the entity invading him. We took turns explaining to the invader that there was a better way to express than through this man, and that the entity could move into the light and really free himself.

At one point Clarence opened his eyes and looked at us. His eyes were clear for a moment, and he recognized us. Then he let out a loud roar and flung his body to a sitting position. His eyes glazed over; we knew that he was not really seeing us. We exerted pressure on his arms, which we still held, and pushed him back on the bed. Again he quieted down and lay unresisting as we continued to talk to the spirit. After approximately half an hour his eyes opened again. He lay quietly as he verbally recognized me, and I introduced him to Freda. After a few minutes of conversation he said he wanted to get up and go into the living room to talk with us. Kathy went to the kitchen and made hot tea for us all. We talked with Clarence for another hour, explaining what had transpired and advising him to have some therapy.

Freda asked him where he had been when he was five. She was picking up that the entity controlling him had attached itself to him at that age, and that it had been in a totally different state than California. After some thought he recalled that his family had visited some relatives in the east when he was small. The relatives ran a boarding house. He remembered that he had been very uncomfortable in that house, and was glad when they returned home. Freda explained that the entity had suffered from malnutrition and physical abuse and died when he was about sixteen. He had attached himself to Clarence because he recognized anger and resentment in the child. This provided him with a physical expression for his own rage.

As we talked, Clarence recalled that as he grew up his mother had remarked that he behaved as if the devil were in him. Kathy said she had thought the same thing when he had fits of rage. These angry spells were infrequent; most of the time he manifested a very mild and friendly manner. He had never been a troublemaker at home or in school. As an adult he was well-liked by his colleagues. However, I had observed many times that his friends made him the butt of their jokes. It was always done in a laughing manner and they included him in all of their activities, but nonetheless he was singled out as different in some indefinable way. I never saw him react with anger to his friends' pranks. He would laugh and seem to enjoy the joke even when it was at his expense. This aspect of his personality will be addressed later as significant to his past.

When Freda and I left Clarence he was tired but felt stabilized and ready for a good sleep. The children had long since hugged their daddy and kissed him goodnight. Kathy explained that they were both close to their children, who seemed to understand that their father had these "sick" episodes and could not help what he did, but that he loved them.

On the way home Freda said she felt we had not succeeded in sending the invading spirit to the light. She was quite certain there was more trouble ahead for Clarence. In the first place, the experience had not dealt with his own problem. He would continue to attract negative energy because of his hidden resentments. He had been an adopted child and, while he loved his parents and they had been exceptionally loving and supportive of him, Freda felt in him a deep resentment toward the mother who had given him up. Because he had been raised in a loving environment he had found little opportunity to express his resentments. His mild and friendly manner apparently was a veneer behind which smoldered considerable rage.

I did not hear from Clarence for about two months. At that point he called and begged me to see him right away — something terrible had happened. I worked him into my schedule that same day and he came in looking very frightened and nervous. He did not waste any time in amenities, but began telling me his experience of the night before.

He had stopped for a drink on the way home from work, to relax his nerves. As he resumed his journey he suddenly felt chills all over his body and sensed that he was not alone. He looked at the seat beside him and saw a devil, dressed in red. This devil said to him, "I have you in my power now and I will never let you go." The apparition disintegrated before his eyes, leaving him with a feeling of sheer terror.

Clarence's religious background was strictly orthodox Christian. He was totally ignorant about reincarnation, regression, and parapsychology. However, he was quite open-minded at this point and ready to try anything I might suggest that would help him. I spent some time explaining my belief system to him and assuring him that he did not have to accept it if he felt uncomfortable with it. If he would be willing to go along with the technique I was about to suggest, which I was sure would help, he could interpret the results any way he wished. He agreed, and very easily achieved an altered state. I asked him where he was. He replied that he was a boy of about seven years of age, in Egypt. The following story unfolded as he described what he felt and saw.

His father had been murdered by three men. His duty as a son was to avenge his father's death, but what could he, a small boy, do to three grown men? He thought on it for a time and devised a plan which worked successfully. He poisoned their food and they all died. He was never apprehended or punished for the deed.

Then I took him to his death in that life. When he died he believed that he had done the right and noble thing in avenging his father. When I asked him to get out of his body and see what his soul's evaluation of that life might be, he was surprised to see that his soul told him he had no right to take those lives. He would have to pay for that and purge his soul of the anger and resentment he still harbored toward those men.

When I asked him to see his purpose in returning to an earth life, and why he had chosen to be adopted, he replied that he had returned to learn the true meaning of love. That was the reason he had chosen such loving adoptive parents, to have an example to emulate, but it had been difficult because of the anger carried over from the past.

He "saw" that his birth mother was unmarried and frightened by her condition. Not in a position to care for a child, and unwilling to have an abortion (which at that time was extremely difficult), she had chosen to give him up for adoption. He "felt" her pain and her love for him, an emotion he cherished, which made it easier for him to release the resentment he had long felt toward her.

Because of the guilt he carried, he felt the need to be rejected in this life. In other words, he believed he was not worthy of acceptance by other people. His rejection began with a mother who gave him up, and followed him throughout his life, right up to the snide and subtle remarks of his contemporaries. He was never really one of the boys. Even in his profession he was a lone worker, although quite successful financially.

This one session in an altered state gave Clarence a very clear and detailed account of his past and how it was affecting his current life. Since he had returned with the express purpose of learning to love and forgive, his own higher knowledge was giving him a "boost," so to speak. He had done a good job of covering up his hostilities and behaving almost always in the gentlemanly manner he had been taught. However, his deep-seated resentments were not only still there, but fostered by the subtle rejection by his peers and the ever-present (though deeply hidden) feeling of being abandoned by his mother.

These feelings had attracted the young entity who took residence in Clarence's energy field when he was a small boy. Each fed on the other's anger, and the invader's power increased with time.

This session gave Clarence considerable confidence in himself. He decided that he could handle the situation with no further help, now that he understood the dynamics of his experience and realized he did not have to be afraid of any "devil." I emphasized the importance of leaving all alcoholic beverages alone, explaining that they robbed him of the capacity to be completely in control of himself. He said he would certainly follow my advice, for he did not want any further confrontations with spirits in any guise.

I did not hear from Clarence for another six months. Then his wife called me again. She reported that he had stopped off for a drink on the way home, thinking that, since nothing unpleasant had occurred in six months, he was now in control. Instead, he was in the hospital with a broken collar bone and a punctured lung.

His story to her was that, after stopping for just one drink, he had resumed his journey. Again he became aware of a presence. This time the steering wheel was wrenched from his hands, and the car ran head-on into a tree. Kathy thought he had learned his lesson this time. He admitted to her that he should have taken my advice. I offered to work with him again to see if we could help him completely release his own resentments. It was clearly evident that he was still carrying anger, and was not free of some sort of invasion.

She reported later that he wanted to do it himself and felt that he could control it as long as he did not drink. Four years later I saw her at the market. She assured me that he had experienced no more problems of a paranormal nature, and that he no longer had the fits of rage which had been so difficult for the family to handle.

In the next chapter two cases will be presented. In the first, the whole problem was handled from a distance and the object of the attack was never aware of the help given him. In the second case, both the attacker and the victim were very human, and they worked out their solution without any outside help.

CHAPTER 17

Two Violent Invasions

Rage Leads to Expulsion

The principal of a middle school in Los Angeles called me one day to discuss a young male student in her school. This woman had never been able to accept the work I did in parapsychology, so her call was especially interesting to me. She was a very religious woman and, although we had been friends over a period of years, she was uncomfortable about my work and we seldom discussed it. However, on this occasion she went into considerable detail about this young boy.

The student experienced spells of rage, during which he was totally out of control. He threw himself on the floor, screamed, banged objects around and at times became completely uncontrollable. His mother had visited the school on numerous occasions, pleading for help of some kind. The spells of rage would occur a number of times in a day; during them he often destroyed objects in the classroom. Under the very capable and caring principal, the school had tried to cooperate with the parents by allowing the boy to remain in class despite his disruptive, uncontrollable behavior.

In spite of help from a private psychologist, the boy's spells seemed to get worse. My friend finally had to suspend him from school. Shortly after his suspension the principal called me. It had suddenly occurred to her that he might be possessed and, knowing my interest in this field, she called for my advice.

Listening to her talk and ask for my help made me feel quite inadequate. There was no way I could see the boy, for neither he nor his mother knew the principal had called me. I finally agreed to think about the problem and consult one of my psychic friends for an opinion.

At that time I was working with a wonderful friend who was not only psychic but also a doctor, with a very large and respectable practice. Her patients had no inkling of her clairvoyant abilities. She and I were meeting one afternoon a week to work in an altered state, asking many questions about life, health, and any other subjects we chose to explore.

When she was in an altered state I presented her with the problem of this boy and asked her to see if she could diagnose his case. With very little hesitation she announced that he was possessed by a malicious entity. The boy literally had no control over his behavior. When I asked her if there was anything we could do to help him, she replied in the affirmative. (This case occurred many years ago, when I was first investigating the paranormal field and knew very little about what to do with invading spirits.)

She assured me that she would follow the instructions given to her by her own spirit guides, and the boy would be freed. I was frankly very skeptical. Nonetheless, she began mentally communicating with the entity in the boy, explaining how it could be free and why it should stop harassing the boy.

I was genuinely astonished when my principal friend called me about a week later. She reported that the boy had stopped having the spells and for the past two days had been normal in his behavior. A few months later this young student had been attending classes regularly with no further incidents.

Deluded by Pseudo-Guides

In another case, my client was receiving messages telepathically and through automatic writing. For the most part the messages purported to be from benevolent spirits who were loving and helpful. She did not consider this experience to be a problem. In fact, she was feeling really special that she had the help of "guardian angels."

However, as she told me about some of the things the voices were telling her to do I became certain that she was being influenced by some very unsavory characters. She and her husband went on a trip. They had gone about seventy-five miles when her voices warned her there was going to be a strong earthquake; if they did not turn back immediately they would soon find the roads impassable and be unable to get back home. Her husband reluctantly complied with her wishes. No earthquake occurred.

She was told not to have sex with her husband. According to the voices, she was now on a spiritual path, and sex would interfere with her development. From our conversations I was quite aware that she did not like having sex; I was certain this so-called spiritual advice was nothing more than her own subconscious wish to avoid sex in her marriage.

On two or three occasions she was instructed to go to a given address in order to meet someone who would be important to her. When she hunted for these places the addresses turned out to be phony.

On her third visit I pleaded with her to refuse to communicate with these voices. I pointed out to her that they were leading her on wild goose chases and actually lying to her. She looked at me condescendingly and said, "You are so sweet to be concerned, but you see, I know my voices. They love me. They use that misinformation to test my loyalty." She believed that she had been especially chosen by a higher power for some kind of important spiritual work. Therefore she must obey without question, and do what she was told to do. No logical arguments on my part made any impression on her firm belief that spirit masters were working through her.

When I asked her why she had come to me, she explained that it was because I was conversant with the paranormal field. She wanted to talk with someone who understood her experience and would not laugh at her. She had many questions she wanted me to answer about parapsychology, but those answers had to fit into her frame of reference or she would not buy them.

After those three visits I did not hear from her for about a month. Then one morning when I answered the phone she was the caller. She reported that she had been in the hospital for the past three weeks. Shortly after her last visit with me she had awakened one night to hear voices screaming in her head. They would not stop. She described the experience as a number of voices all yelling at her at the same time, everyone saying something different. She was unable to quiet her mind or stop the confusion. Her husband took her to the hospital, where they gave her shock treatments.

She assured me that she was now feeling fine; the voices were gone. She apologized for not listening to my advice. She acknowledged that I had been right, that these spirits had intended only to control and confuse her. She said that it had been a terrifying experience, and she was glad it was over, her mind clear and free. I did not hear from her again.

From the literature regarding such experiences, shock treatment is successful because the spirits are literally blasted out of the energy field of the person. In some reports the spirits are very angry when they are subjected to these shocks, for it is very painful to them. Whatever the explanation may be, such an intervention seems to produce the desired results.

In the next chapter my own first encounter with an invading spirit will be discussed. I had read a considerable amount of literature on the subject of possession, but if any of my clients were suffering from this problem I was quite unaware of it. Encountering it for the first time was an unforgettable experience.

CHAPTER 18

My First Encounter with Possession

Henry came into my office looking very ill. He explained that he had been extremely upset for three days; in fact, his energy had been so low he could not go to work. He said he only came to keep his appointment because he thought perhaps I could help him. With a heavy sigh he relaxed on my couch.

The problem seemed to be connected with a visit from his father. He explained that his father lived in another state and had come to spend a few days with him. Unfortunately, he could not stand his father; they had never been compatible. The visit had lasted three days, and he had been miserable all of the time his father was in his home. Although he had not gone to a doctor, he felt like he had the flu. His body hurt, and he felt so tired it was an effort just to walk around.

We discussed his condition. He was inclined to agree with my suggestion that his resentment over his father's visit was responsible for his physical weakness. We decided that this session, which was his third, should be spent in exploring his relationship with his father to help him understand the strong animosity he felt toward him.

However, the moment he reached an altered state he raised up slightly from the couch. In a surprised voice he said, "My God, there is someone else in my body." I was as surprised as he was.

Although I had read about possession, I had never encountered it in anyone I had worked with up to that time. I heard myself saying with complete confidence, "Oh, is that the problem? Well, we can take care of that."

Then, putting all the authority I could manage into my voice, I said, "Whoever you are, you have no right to harass this man and use his body in this way. I command you in the name of God to leave his body at once."

Something grabbed me around the throat; the hair stood up on my arms with a tingling sensation. It was not painful, but the pressure on my throat was strong enough that my voice was somewhat restricted. I continued to speak anyway. "You have no power over me. You have no right to express in this man. In the name of the Father, and the Son, and the Holy Spirit, I command you to leave this house. There is only love here. You must find your own way in your own world."

The restriction on my throat was immediately released. Although I had no proof, since I do not see spirits, I felt that this invader left through a window in the far corner of the room.

My client said simply, "It's gone."

I asked him to remain in the altered state, and we explored the source of the spirit invader. He explained that the spirit had arrived attached to his father. When they argued and my client became angry, the spirit switched hosts. Because the anger was so intense, my client's energy had literally been drained from his body.

At the conclusion of this exploration he sat up. In a relieved voice he said, "This is unbelievable. I feel fine now. My energy feels normal." We briefly discussed his experience, and agreed to work on his relationship with his father at the next session.

Since this was my first encounter with possession I have always wondered why I felt so confident, and was not frightened when the invading energy grabbed me around the throat. I mention this only to point out that my total belief in the power of love and in the rightness of what I was doing seems to be the reason for the effectiveness of my efforts. There was no doubt in my mind that I was more powerful than that spirit, and that it could not hurt me. Conversely, there is much evidence that when the individual is afraid, it can be difficult to get rid of an invading spirit.

Uncontrollable Interference

Matthew was a sales clerk in an auto parts store. One day as he took his sales pad to write up a sale his pen seemed to be jerked out of his control, and he found himself writing nonsense words. He struggled to regain command of his pen. Only after considerable effort did he manage to write up his sale.

For the rest of that day, whenever he started to write up a sale his pen would literally be taken over, and words would be scribbled on his sales pad. It was only by an extreme effort that he was able to write up his sales. A number of times he had to tear off the page and start another. Such words as "pay attention to me," "I want to talk to you," and "listen to me" were written before he could stop them.

By the end of the day he was in a state of confusion, and went home with a violent headache. His wife advised him to make an appointment with me. They had heard me lecture and thought I might be able to help him. However, he was embarrassed that he could not control himself. He decided he would meditate about it and trust it would not happen again.

The next morning his first sales went without incident. After that his pen shook violently again, and he had to throw away two sales slips before he could control the writing. He began to feel real fear and wondered if he was going crazy. He became so unnerved that he had to leave work and go home shortly after his lunch hour.

He had been attending some meetings with a group of people interested in psychic phenomena. They had been experimenting under the leadership of a woman who had read a book on hypnosis and decided to try it with this group. He thought she might be able to help him so he called her. They had a session in which she did a meditation for his protection.

The next morning as he drove to work he felt quite confident that the problem was now resolved, but on his third sales the pen again resisted his writing. It took all of his will power to make it write up his sales. At the end of this day he decided to call me for an appointment.

This case came shortly after Henry's; I was still quite inexperienced with the phenomenon of possession. I did feel confidence in my new client's ability to know what was going on when he was in a trance state. He was a very good subject and reached an altered state in just a few moments.

What he saw was that he was quite psychic, although he had not realized this. During one of the meetings of his psychic phenomena group, the amateur hypnotist had invited spirits to communicate with the group. One of them had attached itself to Matthew. This particular spirit was not malevolent in any sense of the word, just interested in communicating some ideas to human beings. The spirit realized that a person as highly sensitive as Matthew could receive messages the spirit felt were important through automatic writing.

A word of explanation seems appropriate here. Often people die with what they consider unfinished business, or they may espouse a cause of some kind that they believe is very important. When they die they have a compulsion to complete their project, so they attempt to accomplish it through controlling a sensitive individual. This type of invasion is not uncommon. The person involved is often impressed by the entity to such an extent that he takes on its thoughts and feelings and makes them his own.

There seems to be evidence that this type of control is responsible for the radical behavior of certain people, and groups of people, who become over-zealous in promoting their causes.

In the altered state, Matthew made it clear in no uncertain terms that he would not cooperate with this particular spirit entity in any way. He asked the entity to leave him and make no further attempts to communicate with him. This approach to the problem proved to be successful. Matthew's pen no longer wrote anything other than that directed by his own conscious desires, including his product sales slips.

Psychic attack is not always directed from the spirit world. In chapter 19 two case histories will explore the type of invasion that can occur when a human being deliberately directs negative energy to another person. In one case the invasion was planned by a man who had studied mind control in India, and knew exactly what he was doing to his victim. The other case is an example of the harm that can result when an individual who is angry at someone thinks vengeful thoughts.

CHAPTER 19

Mental Invasion on the Physical Plane

This case came to my attention as part of one of those interesting, synchronistic experiences that makes one wonder who is directing the scenario. Louise's mother had recently died, leaving a sizable fortune to be divided between her favorite charities and her alma mater. She had specifically cut her son from her will and made Louise the executrix of her estate. A modest sum was designated for Louise. According to his mother's standards, the son had lived a dissolute life, and she was determined that he should not have any of her money to squander on his lifestyle. He had traveled widely and spent a considerable amount of time in India, studying mind control.

He had tried to talk his sister into breaking their mother's will and giving him a sizable portion. Louise did not want to break the will. Furthermore, by law and because of the arrangements their mother had made, she did not have the power to change it. Her brother was furious with her and began to mentally harass her. When that proved unsuccessful he began working on her son. One day the son stood in the middle of the floor with both hands on his head, screaming, "Get out of my head, get out of my head!" He was so distraught he could not concentrate on his studies. He was a third-year college student, and studying was a full-time job.

When this occurred his mother realized something must be done and got in touch with me. (Louise's nephew had suggested she call me after hearing me speak on parapsychology at his high school.) I told Louise that there was not too much we could do over such a distance, so she made arrangements the next day to fly to Riverside with her son. As soon as they arrived, Gertrude came to my house and the four of us began to work on their problem.

Louise was very frightened. Her efforts to ward off the impressions that came into her mind were quite useless. The most difficult image was of snakes. She had a real fear of snakes, and apparently her brother was aware of this. The most common image she had to deal with consisted of snakes slithering around her body. This impression came into her mind at least once a day, sometimes both morning and evening. At other times she received no clear image, just a feeling of confusion, occasionally accompanied by a roaring in her head.

Gertrude's wonderful clairvoyant gift was of great benefit to Louise and her son. To receive confirmation of their experiences and the assurance that they were not losing their minds was extremely beneficial and reassuring. We spent that first interview answering questions, explaining the dynamics of their situation, and discussing what measures could be taken to alleviate their problem. We were very frank in telling them that there was little any of us could do to stop the mental bombardment. However, there were a number of things Louise and her son could do to combat the attacks.

Since Louise was the prime target, her son felt strong enough to return home and handle the situation on his own. He was concerned about missing school. After two days of working with us he was convinced that there was nothing wrong with his mind, and understood that he could block out the energies directed at him. His mother remained for more work with us. Later reports concerning the son were encouraging. He was still aware of harassment, but found he could turn it off quite successfully.

Louise was not so fortunate. We taught her how to reject thoughts that she felt were not hers. Being very fond of music, she found that when she felt attacked she could sit down and listen to a favorite piece of music. If she concentrated on hearing the notes, her mind would be free of the unwelcome images in a few minutes. Reading something really funny or engrossing was another exercise which helped to focus her mind away from the images.

We explained how the power of love could change people. If she could not change others around her, at least she would be in a better energy field. We instructed her to concentrate daily on the image of a bubble of white light surrounding her completely. She was to visualize any energies directed at her encountering that protective bubble and falling to the ground, unable to reach her. We cautioned her not to send the negative energies back to her brother with anger or resentment, for in so doing she would hold those negative energies in her own auric field.

After five days of practicing mind control and gaining the confidence she needed to proceed on her own, Louise returned home. We kept in touch with her and often spent long hours on the phone, helping her deal with her problem. For a while the situation would seem to improve; then, without warning, the invasion would increase to such a degree that she would have a few bad days.

This struggle between Louise and her brother continued for approximately two years. She had to work every day to keep her mind in control. As she struggled with this problem, she discovered that it was easier to still her mind and relax when she could keep the fear out of her thoughts. Then the pressure would build up again and, as her weariness and stress increased, fears would begin to creep into her mind. These were the most difficult times for her in her mental battle with her brother.

Then an event occurred which gave her evidence that she was not creating illusions out of her own fear. For many months she had been awakened at 5:00 in the morning. Sometimes it was difficult to relax enough to go back to sleep. Then the energy which had been disturbing her at 5:00 stopped. It came at 6:00 instead, with exactly the same intensity and visions, but an hour later. As she puzzled over this she realized that the change to Daylight Savings Time — which requires setting your clocks ahead one hour — had coincided exactly with the change in the disruption of her sleep.

In a phone conversation approximately three years later, Louise assured us the problem had finally come to an end. She no longer felt that her brother was interfering in her life.

A Near Fatal-Attack

For a number of years I taught classes in parapsychology at the YWCA, and for the Parapsychology Association of Riverside, Inc. I always made it a point to encourage class members to ask questions. One evening, a middle-aged woman asked me if one person could kill another with their thoughts.

This can be a dangerous question. I know it is remotely possible. In some societies the authorities have recorded many cases of such killings. However, to give an affirmative answer to a group of inexperienced people could be very frightening, to say the least. Such cases in our culture are so rare as to be almost nonexistent. Therefore, I countered by asking her to explain why she had asked the question.

She said that a friend of hers had apparently been made very ill as a result of death wishes directed at her. In answer to further questions she related a strange story; about halfway through her narrative she confessed that the events were part of her own experience.

She and a friend had an ugly verbal quarrel. As the friend left she shouted, "You'll pay for this! I wish you were dead." The incident left her with a very unhappy feeling. She suffered from a headache and a feeling of weakness following the quarrel. A few days later she experienced violent pains in her abdomen. When the pains in her abdomen became so acute she could not tolerate them, her husband took her to the hospital.

After a series of tests the doctors were unable to diagnose her problem. They could find nothing seriously wrong. However, she continued to get worse, losing strength rapidly. On the third day after her admission to the hospital the doctor could not reverse her condition, and told her husband he did not expect her to live through the night. He suggested that the husband bring their children for a last visit with their mother.

The family gathered around her bed, looking helplessly at their mother's pale and listless face. Too weak to converse with them, she uttered a few faint, endearing words. After they had gone she lay on the bed, wondering what was happening to her. Why was she dying? She seemed to drift in and out of sleep, vaguely aware of a heavy cloud around her.

At about 1:30 in the morning she felt a surge of energy flowing through her body. It shocked her wide awake. She sat up in bed and looked around the room, which was empty. Her feeling of weakness was gone. Just to be sure, she turned her body and stepped out of bed. Three days of lying prone in bed had made her a little unsteady, but a few steps around the room convinced her that something miraculous had occurred. She did not feel any pain; in fact, she felt well.

The next morning she dressed and went home to her amazed but joyous family. Although she puzzled over the experience for a number of days, she could find no solution. Approximately two weeks later, the friend with whom she had quarreled rang her doorbell and asked if she could come in.

Her first words were, "I have come to ask your forgiveness. Please hear me out." She then confessed that she had been so angry she had actually prayed that her friend would die. Then she learned that her prayers were being answered and the object of her attack was in the hospital. At first she was glad her friend was suffering. Later, however, when she heard that her victim was not expected to live, she was filled with remorse, horrified at the monstrous thing she had done.

At exactly 1:30 in the morning she began praying for the recovery of her friend. She was glad when she heard the news of the recovery, but still felt that she had to confess and ask for forgiveness. It had taken her two weeks to work up enough courage to call on her friend. They reconciled at once; each accepted part of the blame for the violent quarrel that had started this unusual scenario.

Needless to say, the class reacted to this woman's story with stunned silence, followed by an explosion of questions. A few were genuinely frightened at the idea that one individual could have that much power over another. The story provided a valuable learning experience for everyone.

I explained that no one has the power of life or death over another individual in the mental dimension. Such an experience could only occur if the right energy conditions made it possible. In this particular case, the mental state of the victim was such that she was vulnerable to the bombardment of her friend. She also was feeling anger and guilt, thus creating ideal conditions for psychic attack. Had she known the source of her illness, it would have been possible for her to heal herself by sending love and forgiveness to her friend.

As we become more aware of the power of the mind to control life and the environment around us, it is of paramount importance that we recognize that an ethic of responsible conduct is essential if we are ever to have a peaceful, creatively productive society.

Psychic power can be used with perfectly good motives, yet still have devastating effects on unsuspecting people. A brief example of this misuse comes to mind. A very dear friend of mine married a doctor who was also a metaphysician. All of her family and many of her friends were very upset. They were all fundamentalist Christians, and the idea of her marrying a man whom they did not consider Christian was very distressing to them.

Shortly after their marriage she began to feel very nervous and tired all of the time. This condition became so disruptive that she could not work. She finally begged her husband to help her find out what was wrong. Since he was also clairvoyant he did some meditating for his wife. He told her that her whole congregation was praying for her to leave him and return to what they considered her rightful place.

She confronted some of the leaders of her church and told them, in no uncertain terms, to leave her alone and stay out of her life. She made it very clear that she had no intention of leaving her husband, nor of ever returning to that church. The problem ended there, and her health soon returned to normal.

In this case the intention of her former church friends and family was not evil. They simply did not realize that they had no right to decide what was right for her. In that sense their act was contrary to spiritual law. Of greater importance, it was totally out of harmony with her wishes and intentions. Their actions created disharmony, first in her auric or energy field, then reflected in her physical organism.

Had my friend been totally loving, she might not have been vulnerable to their prayers. However, no human being is perfect. It is the negativity in all of us that makes outside interference possible. My friend probably carried some guilt for leaving her family and the congregation in which she had been raised. She did have a temper, so I suspect that she had some hidden anger from something in the past.

There is a positive side to all of this interaction on two levels. Were we not sensitive to the thoughts and feelings of other human beings, it would be a cold and harsh world indeed. However, we are constantly affected by the energies put out by the people around us. We must take responsibility for the thoughts we generate. By keeping our own energies commensurate with concern for others, we will avoid much of the negative influence so prevalent in the environment we share.

Chapter 20 will address the role played by discarnates in addictions and crime. While the two problems are separate in society, the underlying motivation is the same. The tormented entity attaches itself to addicted individuals and criminals in order to express its own frustrations and insatiable needs.

Psychic Attack in Addictions, Crime, and Curses

Earlier it has been implied that earthbound entities are present everywhere, constantly seeking opportunities to express their frustrations and meet their needs. The drug addict and the alcoholic are prime targets for these invaders. If these spirits have suffered from either of these problems their influence on the physical person is compounded. Their desires are just as strong as they were when they occupied a physical body. They are in constant emotional pain, existing in a dimension where their desires cannot be met. When they can impress an individual to drink more, or to use drugs, they do exactly that. Since their need is insatiable, there is no end to their control.

Possession vs. Obsession

Some victims are possessed and some are obsessed; there is a difference. The dictionary describes obsession as the influence of a feeling, an idea, or an impulse that a person cannot escape. In the case of obsession, the person responds to urges that come from the outside. In the case of possession, a spirit dwells in the physical body with the soul that belongs there. The spirit has the ability to take over and totally control the individual.

Strong evidence exists which suggests that, in some cases, a number of spirits can possess the same person. In such instances the human sufferer may be very confused and subject to unpredictable behavior. One reads of situations in which the victim insists that voices tell him to commit certain acts. Such people cannot help themselves.

Children Responsive to Invasion

Children are often the victims of this type of control. The emotional problems unique to children must also be taken into account. Some of the unacceptable behavior of children should be attributed to their anger and rebellion against the adults in their world. However, certain types of behavior are particularly suspect. When they occur, possession should not be ruled out as an explanation.

Setting fires is one symptom of possession in children. These children seldom know why they start fires. Sometimes they say that something told them to do it. Unreasonable fits of rage, especially when the child is quite pleasant most of the time, are frequently indications of possession. Kleptomania is another manifestation of spirit invasion, particularly in children who do not need to steal in order to have the things they want. Here again the children are unable to explain their behavior.

If the truth were known, or the causes could be examined, it is quite conceivable that the negative behavior of children is frequently the result of spirit manipulation. Based on what we think we know about psychic attack, discarnates are not allowed to interfere in human affairs except under certain conditions. One of those conditions is determined by the kind of energy that the human being generates. In other words, if a person is angry, carries resentment, or harbors a deep sense of guilt (which is an open invitation for punishment), entities who themselves still carry these negative emotions are attracted to the person.

Since many children are abused, to the extent that they live in a constant emotional state of rebellion and anger, it would be logical to assume that they could serve as surrogate objects for angry spirits. Their energy would attract entities whose own insatiable rage cries out for physical expression. This is not to imply that children do not misbehave out of their own frustrations and rebellion. Each individual comes into this world with a built-in personality. If that personality is loving and kind, mistreatment by parents brings out a different type of behavior than would be manifested by a child who comes in with an angry personality.

I recall a physician who, after the delivery of a male child, said to his wife, "I feel sorry for his parents. He came in filled with rage. I could see it in his eyes." All of the evidence I have seen has led me to the conclusion that every person is born with a built-in destiny. Each personality is the result of centuries of accumulated experiences.

This in no sense negates the psychodynamics of human behavior. Rather it adds a dimension to our understanding of behavior. Psychology at the present time attributes most, if not all, of our emotional problems to the treatment we as children received at the hands of our parents. The multiple-birth philosophy extends the causes of current behavior farther back in time.

An example of this was provided by one of my clients. Her former therapist had succeeded in convincing her, against her better judgment, that her father and her brother were responsible for her difficulty with her husband. After discovering the connection with her husband in a life in Jerusalem under the Roman government, at the end of which she was killed in the arena, she sat up and stated emphatically, "Thank God I don't have to blame my brother and my father any longer. Now I know why I have this problem with my husband." Incidentally, that insight brought a resolution of the problem.

Children do not, as most people believe, come into this life with a clean slate upon which is to be written the events of one life. If such were the case, except for genetic patterning of course, one would indeed arrive here an innocent child, ready to be molded by the environment. This theory is totally inadequate to account for the facts as we see them in the lives of individuals. My file is full of accounts of children who have been beaten, sexually molested, suffered illnesses and accidents, but who still emerged as loving, caring, service-oriented adults. They carry pain but no resentment, no desire to get even with their persecutors. Why this wide gap of responses to the same treatment? The situation calls for a more adequate explanation than our current psychological disciplines offer.

Current Belief Systems Inadequate

A major gap exists in our understanding of the response of individuals to life. It is not easy to describe or understand within the framework of our current belief system. However, if we add the spiritual dimension, the situation becomes comprehensible. In my work I can tell the approximate state of a new client's spiritual orientation within a few minutes. If a client states that forgiving is a forbidden subject, that she has no desire to forgive her father, I know that she is not very far along in her own spiritual understanding. If she says she hates her parents, is very unhappy about this, wants to forgive them, but just can't, I know she has an active spiritual insight and really wants to change her attitude. With such a person, results from regression therapy are generally very successful.

If we are drawing the right assumptions, life is a series of alternate physical and spiritual experiences. Based on available evidence, communication between the two planes is probable, and it is reasonable to expect the influence of one dimension on the other. Stated another way, if everything is energy, as physics now claim, and an intelligence in the form of a mind directs that energy, there should be no problem in a two-way communication. Since it has been well-established that like attracts like, minds and/or emotions in a physical body that are charged with negative energy will obviously attract the same type of negative energy from the non-physical dimension. Minds and emotions in a physical body that are loving, have integrity, and express unselfish intentions are going to attract contacts with entities who possess these same attributes.

Evidence of Psychic Attack in Crime

On the subject of psychic attack in alcoholism and crime, no proof exists that alcoholics and criminals are controlled by entities. I have never personally had a client of either group whose behavior I could positively diagnose as being the result of psychic attack. However, I have read in the media and seen on television many cases where the evidence seems to warrant that explanation.

One such case comes to mind which was widely publicized in the newspapers a few years ago in Southern California. A young father was home with his two small children, ages one and three. His wife was at work. When she returned home she found the baby dead and the three-year-old badly burned. The father had placed his children on the floor heater until they were practically cooked. For two days he maintained that God had made him do it.

172

He believed that the children were evil and possessed, and that he had to drive the devil out of them. Later, after he seemed to recover from this delusion, he went into total denial. He declared he had not done it, and he tried in a number of different ways to kill himself. At his trial he was declared to be mentally deranged and committed to a psychiatric facility, where he is still incarcerated.

I also recall two or three cases of mass shootings in the Los Angeles area in which the killer insisted he could not help himself, that something made him do it.

In such cases, even if spirit control or psychic attack could be accepted as the explanation for the crime, it does not mean that the perpetrator of the crime is innocent. At the present time the law excuses the criminal if it can be proven that he/she was mentally ill at the time the crime was committed. A deep probing into the full dynamics of the cases might well reveal that hidden negative emotional states of the criminals ATTRACTED the discarnate entities who controlled them. At this stage of the total scenario, the individual is responsible for his/her own rage, resentments, or guilt. Nurturing these negative feelings inadvertently provides ideal conditions for invading entities bent on expressing their own destructive emotions. In that sense, the perpetrator IS responsible, even though at the moment of the criminal act he or she was subject to outside control.

Obviously, the central question is not establishing responsibility for criminal acts. In the final analysis, the individual who committed the crime must be held accountable at some level. However, it should not be a matter of punishment for these individuals. The day must come when the dynamics of psychic attack are understood. In the place of punitive measures, the law will provide rehabilitation in the form of genuine, loving concern.

This may sound like an impossible dream. Without a doubt, it will be a long time before it can be realized. However, I believe there are many indications in our society today that such a program has already begun.

There are enough cases on record that prove the efficacy of such a program, and suggest that it might be a realistically practical possibility. For instance, Starr Daily provides an excellent example of the power of love to change individuals. He was condemned, on death row, and had a very unsavory record. Yet he was totally rehabilitated and was pardoned. Afterwards he wrote inspirational books and spent his life lecturing and working for a better world.

Curses

In discussing invasion, one other type of attack should not be ignored: "curses," particularly the kind that are placed on places and objects. Curses, common in many primitive societies and still practiced in some nations today, provide a whole field to be explored. I do not wish to deal with them here, except to note that they are very real, and are not limited to "undeveloped" nations. The case cited in chapter 19, "A Near-Fatal Attack," provides an example of the power of curses.

The type of curses I do wish to mention are those put on places and objects, which affect individuals who come into contact with them. Perhaps some of the most well-known are the curses associated with American Indian sacred grounds. When such areas are disturbed, the individuals responsible often suffer strange illnesses, even death. The curse of the Egyptian mummies is another example. Such incidents occur even in Los Angeles. A chair in an antique store was said to be cursed: whoever sat in that chair was supposed to die within thirty days. Over the brief period of time I followed this story, seven people who had sat in that chair died. One was struck by a car within hours of sitting in the chair, one drowned, and one choked to death. The other deaths were caused by circumstances which I do not recall. It was an especially interesting story because the owner of the store had warned everyone about the chair, but these particular individuals declared they did not believe in curses, and stated that they would prove such things were nonsense by sitting in the chair.

One of my friends bought a second-hand piano bench. From the day it came into her house she felt uncomfortable, although for some days she had no idea what was causing her distress. She finally realized that whenever she got within a few feet of this bench she had strange, eerie feelings and felt nauseated and dizzy. She finally called for psychic help. The psychic picked up at once that it was actually the bench that was causing her discomfort. An entity did not want anyone to have the bench, which had been hers, and so she put a "curse" on it. The psychic took the bench home and spent a number of hours "clearing" it of the negative energy.

What actually occurred here? Was that entity still with the bench, or did she leave a negative energy form around the bench so that anyone near it would be uncomfortable? The psychic who worked with the bench did not pick up an entity, only an energy or force field that had to be dissipated. This would indicate a curse, rather than a direct attack by an entity.

Curses, then, are negative energies deliberately placed around an object or a place to protect it from invaders of all kinds. An interesting question arises here: is the energy totally impersonal, so that it acts on anyone whose energy comes in contact with it? Or is the originator of the curse actually guarding the object and "punishing" any intruder?

In this regard I remember a client I had a number of years ago who had numerous emotional problems. One problem was that she never felt that she was whole, but that some part of her was somewhere else. She could not explain this feeling. Throughout her life she tried to ignore it, but the sensation had an uncomfortable way of intruding on her life and making her feel incomplete. In addition, she explained that in some indefinable way she always felt she was hiding something that she could not tell anyone about.

We decided to try a regression. On the third session she was suddenly in an Egyptian tomb. My questions elicited the following story. She was a trusted servant to the Pharaoh. When he died, she was placed in his tomb to guard it for all eternity. Her death came finally from starvation in the sealed tomb, but her assignment to guard the Pharaoh was a sacred trust and had to be honored. We also had considerable difficulty in getting her to talk about it because she ("he" at that time) had been sworn to silence. In the regression we had a lengthy discussion before she was convinced that she no longer needed to leave a part of herself in that tomb. When she finally accepted the idea that her ancient Egyptian belief need not hold her captive any longer, she was able to release herself from that vow. The results were quite gratifying; she no longer was troubled by feelings of separation and responsibility.

We can speculate for a moment on another aspect of this story. If that tomb had been invaded, would she have caused problems for the invaders? No doubt her spirit would have tried to carry out her promise to protect the Pharaoh.

I will cite one more case from my own experience. We have five colleges or universities in our community. In one of them there are a number of covens, some of which practice witchcraft in its more ugly form. Throughout the past ten years I have had a few calls from young women who were involved in this subculture and became so frightened they called for help.

In one case the group became angry at a young woman who told them she would not be back to their meetings. She began experiencing blackouts and such violent nausea that she would be incapacitated for hours. She finally called me from a phone booth, so terrified that she would not leave until we came for her. I called Gertrude to help me. When the young woman got in my car she sat between us, shaking, her teeth chattering.

We do not know how the group contrived the details of their persecution of this young woman. She would go into a restroom and find a yellow rose on the counter. She would walk into a store and see a vase containing a yellow rose. She was constantly encountering yellow roses, and every time she saw one she would experience the nausea and dizziness, and at times almost faint. This was the form of the "curse" the members of the group had placed upon her. Their power lay in the concentration of the group mind directed at her.

Fortunately we were able to help her. She was a very good person, and once we convinced her that the others had no power over her which she did not allow, she was able to block out their attacks. Gertrude also worked at negating the energies directed at her.

Any reader who wishes to pursue this particular aspect of the subject will find plenty of material on curses. They can be found in all cultures, including our sophisticated, "scientific" modern world.

The next chapter will address the subject of channeling. This word has replaced the long-used term "mediumship." Channeling has become a popular pastime in many metaphysical groups, and a number of recent volumes have been published delineating its virtues and its champions. Some of the varying opinions regarding this phenomenon, its reliability, its sources, and its possible negative aspects, will be discussed.

CHAPTER 21

Is Channeling a Form of Invasion?

By the very nature of the meaning of channeling, the answer to that question must be "yes, channeling is a form of invasion." However, there are many different reasons for communication between the two dimensions. It can be beneficial to humanity, or it can be very destructive. Perhaps the better question would be, is channeling an invasion, or a cooperation?

American Spiritualist Movement

Spiritualistic seances are recorded in the most ancient records. Detailed accounts of paranormal physical phenomena date back to at least the fourth century A.D. In the United States, records from as early as 1830 mention itinerant mesmerists traveling the countryside holding seances, giving messages to the curious, and even prescribing remedies. They claimed to magnetize individuals, giving them special powers.

One of the most famous of the clairvoyants to emerge from these mesmeric practices was Andrew Jackson Davis, often called the John the Baptist of Spiritualism. In the early 1840s his demonstrations startled audiences wherever he appeared.[1]

However, the Spiritualist movement as a religion started at a particular time and place: 1848, in Hydesville, New York. John

Fox had six children. In 1848 two of his daughters, Maggie and Kate, began hearing sounds which seemed to come from the walls. At first they were terrified, but soon they discovered that the raps would respond to their requests and answer questions. Their mother joined the fun, and answers were tapped out for her which were so accurate their authenticity could not be questioned.

Neighbors and friends soon joined them in "sittings." From this humble beginning the Spiritualist Church emerged as a powerful influence. The movement spread rapidly across the country. Thousands of small groups met in dimly-lit rooms to invite the spirits to manifest. In many such groups someone would discover they possessed clairvoyant ability and could communicate with the spirits. Often such an individual would spontaneously lapse into a trance state and produce information which was unknown to the sitters. Such trance mediums had no memory of their experience. They often remained in a slightly dazed and confused state for a brief period following their trance.

The Fox family suffered considerable persecution, including damage to their home from rocks thrown by frightened citizens who were convinced the family was controlled by the devil. In spite of support from many influential people, their lives were never free of harassment. Many years later, they accepted a large sum of money to admit that their manifestations were fraudulent. They were reluctant to make such a false confession, but they reasoned that they needed the money. They had been persecuted for a lifetime; no one believed their story, so why not make some profit for themselves at last? However, their false confession had little influence on the Spiritualist Movement. Too many others who followed them demonstrated the reality of a power from another dimension.

In addition to trance-speaking, some of the early mediums possessed remarkable powers of levitation and demonstrated the ability to move heavy objects. Typology, commonly known as table-tipping, was another favorite pastime among the devotees.

William Stanton Moses, a clergyman and teacher, was a spiritualist famous for his feats. He was said to have a group of spirits working through him. Daniel D. Home was probably the most remarkable of the physical mediums. He levitated and moved his body through space in the presence of witnesses. Outside of the trance state he had total amnesia regarding the events that occurred.[2]

Although many researchers endeavored to prove that Home's manifestations were fraudulent, all of them were forced to conclude that his amazing feats were genuine. He demonstrated under any conditions, and did not require the darkened room that was a common setting for seances.

Mrs. Leonore Piper was another medium who was studied and investigated by numerous skeptics over a period of many years. Her reputation remained untarnished by fraud.[3]

These early trance mediums were totally taken over and controlled by their spirit guides. When the trance period terminated they had no recollection of what transpired or what they said. Many of them possessed this ability at a very young age and tried to ignore it, but often they would go into spontaneous trances, sometimes against their will. In some cases the parents were considerably distressed over this behavior in their children, believing they were devil-possessed. At any rate, many of the early mediums seemed to be pushed into this activity by a force outside of themselves.

This early period of spiritualism fascinated many people, and drew violent rejection from many others. One wonders if the personalities in that other dimension might not have engineered a concerted drive to break through the fear and ignorance which has gripped humanity for so long. Perhaps they concluded that it was time to prove their existence and finally relieve humanity of some of the fears regarding the reality of spirits. Certainly the spiritualist movement has done this for vast numbers of people.

The old must ever give way to the new. When mediumship lost much of its public appeal, suffering considerable rejection because of its many charlatans, channeling emerged on the scene. No longer was it necessary to go into a trance to communicate with the spirits. Large numbers of people discovered that they could experience contact with intelligent minds outside of themselves.

Fraudulent Practices

Fraudulent practices damaged the image of many mediums from the beginning of the spiritualist movement. Even the most talented could not always produce messages and phenomena, so trickery became a common occurrence. Before long every medium was suspect. When confronted with their dishonest practices, many mediums maintained that they were bringing comfort to the bereaved; with the use of "props" their clients would never be disappointed. According to their point of view, if they failed they were called frauds and their customers were disappointed, but if they satisfied their clients, everyone went away happy.

One of the most detailed exposés of mediumistic fraud can be found in a paperback volume published by Dell Publishing Co. in New York in 1976, under the title *The Psychic Mafia*. In this book, written by M. Lamar Keene, tricks are exposed by individuals within the ranks of the spiritualist movement, lending greater credence to the report.

Fraudulent practices became so common that when Daniel Logan, a gifted clairvoyant, became famous for his demonstrations, he was approached by a distributor of paraphernalia used for creating spirit manifestations. When he indignantly informed the salesman that he was not interested, because his gift was genuine and he did not require artificial assistance, he was told to be practical: "everyone" used the props of the trade. Mr. Logan spent three days with us in Riverside, lecturing and giving individual consultations. I was highly impressed by his humility, and by his dedication to using his gift to help people. His book, *The Reluctant Prophet*, publsihed in 1968 in Garden City, New York, by Doubleday and Co., is an excellent portrait of a genuine medium.

Mediums — Innovators of Spirit Communication

Logan's story also provides an example of the dynamics of one whose destiny seems to be unavoidable. A force, or guidance, from a source outside of himself literally forced him to follow the path of a medium and clairvoyant. He admits that he had little choice in the matter. Is this an example of invasion, or did Logan plan or agree to this destiny before he came into this incarnation? In the latter case either his own "all-knowing mind" directed his development and activity in this field, or a guide or "advisor" from the other dimension, possibly assigned to assist him in carrying out his destiny, guided him into the path he had chosen prior to birth. On the face of it, one has little choice when powers of this kind seemingly take over a life.

A study of the spiritualist movement and its credo reveals the incorporation of the highest principles of Christianity. The many mediums who possess the gift of communication are, for the most part, aware of their strange gift at an early age, and believe that they have no way of avoiding their destiny to serve humanity in this way. Does this imply possession, invasion on the part of a non-physical intelligence? Or does it indicate that some Super-power has determined that human beings are ready to receive indisputable evidence of their ability to communicate with the spiritual dimensions, and therefore has either "drafted" or called for volunteers to incarnate for this purpose?

This last suggestion may sound facetious — but is it? Certainly it is not inconsistent with evidence that indicates that many souls incarnate with pre-arranged destinies to further the progress of humanity in our search for higher creative expression and greater understanding of ourselves.

A study of history seems to point to a simultaneity of ideas emerging in various countries. Hendrick Willen Van Loon's *The Arts*, published in 1937 in New York by Simon and Schuster, delineates this phenomenon, pointing out how various art forms emerged on the scene at the same time in different countries, without the artists having physical contact or communication with each other. Another more recent work by Marilyn Ferguson, *The Aquarian Conspiracy*, published in 1980 in Los Angeles by J. P. Tarcher, Inc., presents a powerful case for the idea that the emergence of worldwide interest in metaphysics is orchestrated by a force beyond the ordinary physical dimension.

Specific individual cases have been cited earlier in which contributions in the form of technical and scientific information have been communicated to men and women with special skills. While some individuals devote their lives to serving as recipients of information from the spirit world, could it be that communication is going on all the time, unrecognized by most recipients? Could it be that when human beings are ready for a new idea, or advanced enough to utilize higher concepts, the spirits are the means by which such information is conveyed to us?

There is certainly a big difference in the *modus operandi* of communication. Is there also a difference in purpose or motive? Many mediums suffered poor health, and over the years deteriorated physically. The explanation has often been advanced that their gift continually drew upon their energies, and their bodies suffered from this constant drain. Why was this true for some mediums, and not for others?

I have been well-acquainted with two spiritual mediums. One suffered over the years from many physical ailments. The other did not and lived to be very elderly. She saw clients on a daily schedule; most of the time her calendar was full, with people waiting. She once told me that when this talent was used properly the medium did not suffer depletion. In fact, she said the spirits who helped her gave her a steady input of energy to replace whatever was expended in working with disturbed people, and she almost never felt tired.

Channeled Healing

I have come to believe that the attitude or belief system of the medium or psychic healer or reader is the primary factor affecting their health. One experience will illustrate this. The Parapsychology Association of Riverside often held public fairs to publicize the Association and to give people the benefit of paranormal skills.

One healer in the organization possessed phenomenal power. I had seen her take the pain from a sprained ankle in five minutes. The ankle became black and blue up into the leg, but there was absolutely no pain. I asked her to help with the fair by demonstrating healing for people who wanted such help. She agreed, on the condition that she see only three people in one day. Her teacher had told her it took too much of her energy if she healed more than that.

I gave her a few words of advice on how she could heal without using up any of her own energy. She simply needed to recognize and believe that energy exists in endless supply, and that she would be replenished constantly as she gave energy to others. The day of the fair she worked with thirty-four people, and helped many of them. She called me the next day to tell me that when she got home after the fair she felt so full of energy she had taken off her shoes and danced on her lawn. She expected the fatigue would catch up with her the following day, but instead she awoke feeling fine.

That may not be an adequate formula for success in all cases. Perhaps the spirit healers who work through the physical body have different levels of development. I know of no healers who claim that they do the healing. All believe that they are instruments through which spirit healers work. Is the difference in the success of healers due to their own spiritual development, or to the level of the development in the entity working through them? Perhaps both are factors in the success of the healing. It may be that the more spiritually developed the healer is, the higher the spiritual energies he/she attracts.

At any event, all of these cases of spirits using human beings seem to involve some very direct control, certainly a type of invasion. When is invasion detrimental and when is it beneficial, a part of the planned pattern of the individual?

Spirit Intervention

One of my early experiences with Gertrude Hall occurred in connection with one of my speaking engagements in the Los Angeles area. At that time she was studying with me to develop her psychic ability. Two days before the lecture I developed a hoarseness which made it difficult for me to talk. My throat did not hurt, but I could not be heard beyond a few feet. Although I tried my usual methods for recovering my voice, nothing was effective. I kept getting a mental message that I should call Gertrude and ask her to go with me, but I told myself that it was not fair to her to ask her to come, since she had never done any public speaking. Then the thought came to me that perhaps this would be a good chance for her to try her psychic skills with a group, something she had never done.

Apologetically, I called her and explained my throat condition. I asked her to go with me and be the speaker. Her reply astounded me. She said, "Why did it take you so long? They (her spirit guides) told me three days ago that you would call and ask me to do this. I have arranged for a babysitter and I am all ready to go with you."

When we arrived at the meeting my voice worked perfectly. I gave a short talk, then introduced Gertrude as a psychic whom I had brought with me to demonstrate psychic ability. I explained that she would answer one question for each person present. We started around the circle. At first Gertrude did an excellent job of answering each question, but then she drew a blank. Although she was quite shaken by this unexpected turn of events, she covered it well. I explained to the group that sometimes people who were rather private could block another mind from getting into theirs, so we would move on to the next person. She was able to answer the questions that all of the other women asked her, and they were very impressed.

On the way home Gertrude exploded. She declared that she would never again put herself in that kind of a situation; it was too embarrassing. I did not argue with her, but the next time she came for a training session, after she was in a deep trance, I asked her to see why she had drawn a blank at the meeting. The answer that came to her was very specific. She was told that she had to understand that her answers came from her spirit helpers. Without them she would not be able to do this kind of work. They had taken this dramatic way to prove it to her so she would not ever forget it, and they pointed out that she need never feel responsible for the answers that came through her. This understanding was to help relieve her of any fears that she might give people the wrong advice.

Her spirit guides also promised that they would never do that to her again. They also took the responsibility for the loss of my voice. When Gertrude protested, they assured her that they would not do that to me again, either. Then they went on to explain that since I have a standing agreement that I am willing to be used in any way that will help others, I was simply cooperating in their efforts to help Gertrude with her development in this field. Gertrude was somewhat mollified, and reluctantly agreed to be guided by them in helping people who sought her advice.

Certainly in this case the invading spirits were benevolent, and in all probability cooperating in a pre-arranged destiny plan for Gertrude. Since she had been psychic from early childhood, she had chosen a program of helping people in this way. From all the evidence we have, it seems that spirit guidance or intervention is the answer to all psychic phenomena.

Channeling

A few years ago the word "channeler" replaced the word "medium" to a large extent. For the majority of channelers communication is very smooth, and reception does not require a deep trance state. Some demonstrate this ability by sitting in front of an audience and going through certain physical contortions as they enter a trance state. Some are aware of everything they say, while others are unaware of the words they utter. In some areas they are all called trance mediums.

A very gifted young trance medium came to me for help with some personal emotional problems. One day when he was in a trance I asked his guide if it was really necessary for him to take the time to go through the facial and neck contortions which established that he was making contact with a spirit. His guide replied, "No, it is not, but he is very good, and this dramatic way of presenting himself impresses an audience. With it, they are more convinced that they are getting messages from the 'beyond.'" Then the spirit said that he would cause the young man to be in a trance state so he would not be aware of what he was saying to me. The voice coming from him then told me some things that were to occur in the young man's future, which he was not ready to know about at the present time. When the session was over, the young man had no recollection of the conversation that had taken place between the spirit and me.

Whether it is good or bad, and regardless of the purpose, it seems to be a fact that spirits do invade our space. They guide or sometimes "push" us into specific behavior and into particular thought patterns. Anyone who is at all familiar with mediumship and channeling will recognize that there is a difference between spiritual guidance and spirit possession, or even obsession.

In the final analysis, then, it would appear that communication between the two dimensions, the physical and the spiritual, is a constant exchange on multitudinous levels spanning the benevolent and malevolent. Our hunches, ideas, inspirations, and intuitions may all come from three possible sources: one, our own higher, all-knowing minds; two, spirit guides; or three, our minds tapping some sort of universal knowledge bank.

This is a disarmingly simple approach to a profound subject. The dynamics of the communication are tremendously involved, but if we postulate a "one universal mind" in which we all interrelate, then mind-energy becomes the *sine qua non* of the entire structure of human beings and our involvement in the life process. It follows, then, that mind operates both in and out of a physical body and is most limited when in the confines of a physical form.

Channeling might be interpreted as a break in the physical barrier. It allows humanity to benefit from the help of more advanced minds. The danger in this communication comes from malevolent entities whose purpose is to create confusion and pain, rather than to give creative support and foster harmony.

The Quality of Communications

What determines the quality of the communications? This becomes a tremendously important question as this interchange increases on the earth plane. The literature on this subject assures us that spirits are bound by spiritual law to respect the free will of human beings. They may not interfere unless conditions are such that their intervention does not violate individual rights.

An experience I had with automatic writing some years ago will serve as an example of this principle. I had decided to use this method of communication as part of my research. At times I received totally false information and a lot of irrelevant material. When I challenged my spirit source (with indignation, I might add), I was told that when I was in an angry mood, or upset about something, they were helpless to reach me and had to stand by and watch me attract negative "stuff." All of my good intentions, and the fact that I was positive most of the time, did not protect me when I lapsed into a negative mood.

My observations over many years of working with clients have convinced me that this is the key. It does not matter how hard one prays, begs, pleads with God, or even gives generously to charities. If rage, resentment, guilt, selfishness, jealousy, and fear exist in the personality, those negative energies are an open door for malevolent entities. When the individual is genuinely loving and unselfishly motivated in whatever niche he/she occupies, whether it be that of a famous surgeon or a devoted mother and wife, the communication from the other plane is going to be totally supportive and beneficial, and it will be there whether it is recognized or not.

How many people stop to wonder how prayers are answered? A beautiful poem begins, "God has no hands but our hands to do His work today. He has no feet but our feet to help people on their way."[4] What could be more magnificent than a universe in which we are all one and so interrelated that we serve the Source, or the Supreme Being, by responding to each other and helping where help is needed?

The following case illustrates this idea. It happened many years ago but I have never forgotten it because at the time, it triggered in me the idea of how we all serve "God." A poor young minister was serving a small country church. He prayed for $100 to pay the physician who would soon be delivering his expected child. He apologized to God for asking for money, but the need seemed to justify the request.

In a neighboring town, about thirty miles away, a woman said to her husband, "I can't seem to get a thought out of my mind. A number of years ago I borrowed $100 from a friend and I just feel

I must repay her. Would you drive me to her home so I can return the money?" The husband complied and the money was repaid.

The woman's friend went to the minister and said, "Pastor, I was just given $100 as payment from an old debt. I do not need the money, but I had a feeling that you could use it for something that is important to you. Will you please accept it as a gift from me ?" The minister gratefully thanked God for the money.

How are such events brought about? I could cite many others from my own experience. The pastor's need and his plea set something in motion, but just how and through what channels was that series of events orchestrated? It is interesting to speculate on the possible explanations for what we loosely term coincidences.

Did the minister's spirit guide contact the spirit guides of the two women, who responded accordingly? Perhaps the minister's mind energy set something in motion in the universal energy "bank." Like a computer, it responded to the order it picked up from his mind. Or possibly his spirit guide directly impressed the two women to respond as they did.

Whatever the answer may be, we can be quite certain from the evidence we have that communication takes place between the two dimensions. This communication is purposeful and beneficial. It is probably an erroneous judgment to state that some of it is bad. If malevolent spirits are attracted by negativity, then that must be a part of the lesson to be learned by those who harbor destructive thoughts. In such cases, invasion or possession unquestionably takes place to the discomfort of the individual, but for the purpose of his or her own spiritual growth.

Channeling, as currently practiced, is just a new word to describe contact with spiritual dimensions, and has been going on probably as long as humanity has inhabited this planet. Because human beings are rapidly moving toward a better understanding of their spiritual nature, communication is becoming recognized as a normal interchange of information and help between minds in all stages of development.

The next chapter will attempt to synthesize the elements of communication and explore the benefits which every individual can derive from an understanding of how to use those elements. We will search for answers to the question: "How can we as humans enhance our lives and resolve our problems through the application of some of the principles inherent in interdimensional communication?" It has been my experience that life can be immeasurably enhanced when certain axioms or universal laws are recognized and followed.

---

1. Douglas Hill and Pat Williams, *The Supernatural* (New York: Hawthorne Books Publishers, 1965), 111.
2. Ibid., 115, and Ronald Pearsall, *The Table Rappers* (London: Michael Joseph, 1972).
3. Willis Harman and Howard Rheingold, *Higher Creativity* (Los Angeles: Jeremy P. Tarcher, Inc., 1984), 139, and Hill and Williams, 121.
4. Author unknown.

CHAPTER 22

Flowing with the Stream
of Consciousness

What does it mean to "flow with the stream of consciousness?" How is that concept related to hauntings or possession? Perhaps it is not, *per se*, but it does very definitely have to do with the energies responsible for contacts from the other plane.

When one flows with the stream of consciousness it is like being tuned in to a guidance system that is infallible. Who supplies that guidance? Where does the information come from? Most people describe the feeling as a hunch, or like someone speaking into their minds. For many this sense of direction is very clear and specific; for others it is vague, more like an idea that originates in their own minds.

Many agree that if they ask for answers the replies they receive are not always accurate. However, if a mental direction or hunch comes suddenly, or unexpectedly, or spontaneously, it is practically always right. Some people credit their guidance to relatives who have died and who, out of love, are still helping them. This seems to be true in certain cases where people are saved from serious accidents, or warned of danger. Such events are quite common.

There seems to be considerable evidence that many who dwell in the spiritual dimension choose to serve as guides to human beings and are assigned to the people they are to help. Chapter 12 cited numerous examples of spirits who apparently had special skills in their lives and who now choose to help humanity by impressing people with advanced information in the fields of science, medicine, and other research areas.

Encounter with a Spiritual Reader

I well recall my first encounter with a spiritual reader. While in my early twenties I was told of a young man who was a spiritualist minister and lived in Santa Monica. I was directed to write out five questions and place them in my bra; he would answer them all. It was difficult for me to believe this but I decided to test it. When I arrived at his home I was ushered into a small, dimly-lit room. He was only seventeen years old, but had chosen to devote his life to this type of work. As I watched his face, he closed his eyes and seemed to go into a short meditation. Then he began to speak. To my amazement he told me my questions in the order in which I had written them, and gave me the answers.

Then he added some other things, including a warning about the man I was to marry. He explained that there would be a money shortage at the bank and everyone would be questioned, including my fiance. This, he said, would be very upsetting to my fiance because of his integrity.

When I returned home I called my friend and gave him the warning. He dismissed it and asked me not to worry about it. He was quite certain nothing like that would happen. For the next few months nothing happened, and he gently chided me for believing fortune tellers. Seven years later, however, the shortage happened just as the young minister had predicted. Later, as I worked with people and helped them develop this talent, I learned that a vision may come in strong and clear because it is emotionally charged. The event may appear to be imminent, but in the physical world it may take place sometime in the future.

Personal Spirit Guides

Many people believe that they have a spirit guide. Individuals who lead busy lives, in which different activities are a part of their daily routine, often have more than one guide. In other words, they may have one guide who advises them when they plan business strategies, another when they are playing in an orchestra as an avocation, and possibly a third when they are doing creative writing.

Some people may think that spirit guides never make mistakes, but their personalities are not altered significantly nor do they become suddenly wise or knowledgeable just because they no longer have physical bodies. Sometimes they cannot work compatibly with the individual assigned to them. I had one friend who was developing her psychic skills. She was given a very strong and wise guide in the early weeks of her training. He not only was helping her in developing her psychic skills, but was assisting her with her children and smoothing out problems in her life in order for her to have time to concentrate and practice her psychic lessons. He was very considerate of her needs. After a few weeks he was replaced by another guide, supposedly a master guide, while he was sent on to someone else in the initial stages of developing psychic skills.

By this time my friend was able to give psychic readings for people, and do a very good job of it. Although the replacement guide was quite skilled and could give her answers to the questions she was asked by people who came to her, he had little understanding of her personal feelings or needs. For example, whenever she wanted her children to come home, the first guide would impress them and they would shortly appear. The second guide was not concerned about helping her with her family problems. He really did not understand why mortals got so upset over things that to him were totally unimportant.

One day she flew into a rage when he had not helped her as she expected. She swore at him and told him to get lost; she would not work with him any longer and she wanted him out of her life. It was quite a surprise to her when he backed off apologetically and said, "I did not know human beings ever talked to spirits like that." The first spirit teacher then returned long enough to apologize to her for sending her a helper who was so insensitive to her personal needs, and she soon received another assistant.

Two-Way Cooperation

There is clear evidence that psychic readers get their information from a *spirit* source, not necessarily a *spiritual* source. Spirits appear to be responsible for the information that psychic readers receive and pass on to their clients. However, by no means are all spirits "spiritual" beings. Spirits are able to communicate with mortals regardless of their own spiritual development. All of the psychics I have known recognize this source and the cooperation required if one is to serve humanity in this way. This explains why some readers are so much more highly skilled and accurate than others. Their own degree of spiritual development determines, in large measure, the quality of the spirit guide they attract.

One often hears the statement that a person can be a good psychic and not spiritually oriented, but that any spiritual person will be clairvoyant. There is a considerable difference in the types of readings done by the two. The former gives readings that deal with mundane subjects such as love problems, accidents, deaths, and money. Spiritually-developed clairvoyants may include some information on these subjects, but their primary concern is helping the individual to put his or her life together, resolve emotional problems, and understand undesirable behavior patterns.

Many sidewalk readers are just very clever people with a keen understanding of human nature. They know how to lead a client into disclosing a great deal of information, which they then rephrase so that it sounds as if they know more than they do. Telepathy also plays a strong role in psychic readings. If the client has a really strong desire for something and asks the reader if that wish will be granted, the reader picks up that desire energy and sees it as materializing.

One case will demonstrate this effect. A woman was in love with a married man who stopped by her house almost every morning on his way to work "to have coffee." For six years he promised her that he would get a divorce as soon as his three children graduated from college. Two years after they graduated he was still making promises and excuses about why he had to wait a little longer.

During those years she consulted many psychics; in fact, every new one she heard about. All of them told her to hang on and she would have him — that is, all except two. Those two told her to forget him. It would never work out for her. When she told me about her problem she indignantly informed me that those two were not good readers. However, a time came when the gentleman did not stop by her house for a few days. She desperately tried to reach him, only to discover that he had sold his house and moved out of town. She called me in a panic and some considerable rage to inform me that all psychics were frauds. I asked her to calm down and listen, and I reminded her that I had advised her many times to terminate the relationship. I had begged her to stop running her life on the advice of psychic readers. I also reminded her of the two readers who had told her she would never have him in a permanent relationship. Then I suggested that the others were picking up her intense desire; they saw it as a reality because that was how she perceived it.

Psychics Are Not Infallible

All psychics are fallible and have varying degrees of accuracy. One of the most famous and highly accurate readers I have known was said to have been accurate eighty-five to ninety percent of the time. I have seen him perform for large audiences numerous times and apparently never miss a question. Of course his predictions could not be checked. He became highly sought-after and ended up in a famous resort where he became part of the fast lane — drinking, partying, and smoking marijuana. In a period of a year his degree of accuracy dropped to close to forty-five percent.

I have intimately known a number of psychics over the years whose lives were totally dedicated to helping people with their clairvoyant talents. They charged minimal fees, or worked on a donation system, often seeing a steady stream of clients five or six days a week. Their clients included business people who depended on them for major decisions in investments; lawyers and judges; law enforcement personnel who usually made inquiries through a third party so they could disclaim any connection with psychics; and the general public.

A psychic with integrity will never claim to be infallible. One explanation for their errors can be found in the spiritual law of free will. Psychics will often say, "If you continue on the path you are traveling now, such and such will happen, but you have free will and can change the future if you choose to do so." Another common cause of errors results from a misinterpretation of symbols. Some psychics receive their information in symbols and fail to understand their meaning.

Whether there is any validity to one explanation for error, or whether it is just rationalization, is anyone's guess. For whatever it is worth, I have another explanation for erroneous readings. More than one psychic, while in trance in a research session, has explained that no one is allowed to be one hundred percent accurate. The responsibility placed on a human being who had that much power would be too awesome to handle. I have accepted this explanation. One has only to consider any person who seemingly never makes mistakes to realize how unpopular they are. Errors are our tools for learning, and every human being makes mistakes. We would not need to be here in a physical body if we were perfect.

Types of Psychic Skills

Because I was continually studying the parapsychology field and seeking a better understanding of the dynamics of paranormal phenomena, I frequently visited psychic readers to observe and test their skills. Although their methods ranged from ordinary playing cards to crystal balls, most of them admitted that these were only props. Their information came through their minds from some source outside of themselves. The spiritualist readers openly recognized their spirit "friends," as they called them, and conversed with the source of their information while giving readings for the client. Card readers would often remark that the cards said "such and such," and they also saw the prediction in vision. Some simply sat with the client and, in a conversational way, related what came into their minds.

I enjoyed the friendship of one psychic reader in San Bernardino for many years and visited her about twice a year. If I went to see her just as a friend, she never failed to insist that she give me a reading. She told me in advance about most of the major changes that occurred in our family — births, deaths, trips, illnesses. I do not recall her ever being wrong, although I thought she was a few times. She told me I would have another child, a son. For a number of years I waited for that baby; he never came. One day I challenged her about it. I was forty-five years old at the time and had not seen her for two or three years. I assured her that she was way off on that prediction. I certainly was not going to have another child at my age, nor did I want to be a mother again.

She puzzled over it a moment and then said, "I am sorry, but I still say you will have another son. It will not be long now. I see him very clearly; he is coming to you." I confess I was quite baffled by this, but not long after that we adopted our baby grandson and, in spite of myself, I became a mother again. The whole thing came about in such a way that my husband and I could not avoid taking on that responsibility. I was convinced that I was definitely supposed to include this child in my destiny.

Personal Advantages of Communication

These cases have been cited to provide the reader with some concrete evidence of the existence of direction and guidance from intelligent beings in the other dimension. But of what value is this to the average person? Not many people want to be psychic readers. However, the fact that communication can and does occur between the physical and spiritual worlds would seem to indicate that all human beings have the potential for this interchange. When the right conditions are met, anyone can have the benefit of help and direction from the non-physical world.

It is of paramount importance to remember that when this communication is used in accordance with spiritual law, it is not control from spiritual entities in any sense of the word. Human beings always have free will to listen or ignore any advice or direction given from outside of themselves. To use an analogy, it is not dissimilar to going to a parent, teacher, minister, or wise friend, and asking for help and advice in some important matter. Their help, no matter how practical or sensible it might be, can be accepted or rejected.

Even in the limited number of clients I see, a large percentage of them, when questioned, can recall evidence of their clairvoyant capacities. They may remember a simple precognitive insight when they were children, or a sense that they have lived before. Most of them mentally discarded their experiences early in their lives because of the cultural rejection they encountered from parents and teachers who made them feel "different" from or unacceptable to "normal" people. When these children chose a destiny in which this talent was to be expressed, considerable pain and often punishment were the price they paid for following their chosen path.

The famous Eileen Garrett is an excellent example. One of the truly great ladies in the paranormal field, she was a successful business woman, earning a living as the owner of a publishing business. At her own expense she traveled to research centers that invited her to be a subject for investigation. When I met her in New York many years ago she graciously gave me over an hour of her time to answer my questions. She told me she had no explanation for her gift. She only knew what she could do; it was up to the scientists to explain it. She had been raised by a very strict grandmother who punished her severely when she was only three for talking about things she "could not know." She learned to be very careful about what she said around adults. As a child she lived in two worlds, and the physical one was very painful. She is a beautiful example of the gifted souls who have come to dispel the fear and superstition surrounding the spirit world.

Benefits of Flowing with the Stream of Consciousness

With the understanding that there is an endless source of help available to all of us if we ask and listen, I would like to address the theme of this chapter. Exactly what do I mean by the phrase, "Flowing with the Stream of Consciousness?" It is a matter of living constantly with an awareness that help and advice are always available to you, and that you are free to respond accordingly.

You can be Christian, Moslem, agnostic or atheist. If you pray for help sincerely and earnestly, there is someone "out there" who is going to try to help you. Barriers often prevent their help from coming to you. One of these is your own guilt. If people feel unworthy of good coming to them, their prayers are not going to be answered. They cannot be, because the individual has set up a barrier to their accomplishment. Therefore one of the criteria for success is loving yourself and knowing that you are worthy of this relationship.

No one is perfect, nor can we be. As human beings we all have a dark side which manifests in the daily vicissitudes of living. Our motives are the measure of our success. If our motives are unselfish, service-oriented, free of greed, free of the need for aggrandizement and other destructive, negative emotions, our help from the other plane will be more readily available, and of a higher quality.

It is important to understand that this kind of help does not imply that any individual can escape the responsibility of overcoming the emotional blocks to spiritual awareness. A spirit guide may lead you to a parking space when you go shopping, but be quite unable to answer your request for healing if you are manifesting high blood pressure because of your rage at an employer or a spouse. Working on the negative blind spots in our own personalities, such as egocentricity, selfishness, greed, jealousy, and arrogance, requires our constant attention.

Only by being aware of the feedback from our bodies and our articulate friends can we recognize that we are out of harmony and need to make some changes. When we honestly seek answers and are ready and willing to make some changes, even though our pride may suffer, assistance from the spirit guides will be forthcoming. It may come in the form of a book that you feel impelled to buy or borrow. It may come through a friend who invites you to a lecture at which you hear something that gives you insight. It can come from psychological counseling, and it is almost sure to come if you go through regression therapy.

The benefits from living daily with the consciousness of being in that flow are legion, and include every aspect of life. If you lose or misplace something, you simply ask where it is. The answer may not come instantly, and you may not find the object at once. It depends on the urgency of the request.

One of my own experiences illustrates this. I picked up my purse and reached for a letter that I had left on my desk. I was on my way to a meeting where I had to read that letter. It was not there. For a moment I was quite frantic. To go to the meeting without the letter was going to place me in a very embarrassing position. I hurriedly turned over the papers on my desk, but the letter was not there. Then I stopped, closed my eyes and said, "Okay, I do not have time to hunt for this. Where is it?" Immediately the name of one of the files in my cabinet came into my mind. Although that file had no relevance whatever to the letter, I opened the drawer and lifted out the folder. I hurriedly thumbed through the papers. About five pages down the letter came into view.

I realized that earlier in the day someone had come in for some information and I had taken out that file. In returning it I had picked up the letter, which was on the bottom of the other papers. I grasped it gratefully, picked up my purse and headed for the door, lifting my eyes heavenward for a moment to say, "Oh, thank you, thank you very much." I received an instant, unmistakable mental response, as clear as if someone was standing beside me. "We could do that for you all of the time if you would just listen." Needless to say I was delighted, and it certainly did help me to pay more attention.

A quite different experience occurred when I was asked for the name and address of a certain individual. I did not have it and I was not sure how I could procure it, but I had met this person and would recognize her if I saw her. I was attending classes at UCLA at the time and always sat in the back row, on the aisle. On this particular evening I started to sit in my usual seat and literally could not sit down there. I started down the aisle and attempted to stop three times, but something kept propelling me forward. I finally sat down and as I settled into the seat, the person in front of me and one seat to the left turned around. It was the woman whose address I wanted.

As this constant guidance manifests in so many practical ways, one gets used to it, until it becomes an integral part of life. It is expected, and it is not questioned, because it is always right, even when it seems unreasonable. I recall one incident involving guests who brought their baby to our home. When they were ready to leave, we could not find the baby's blanket. Everyone in the house was looking for that essential item. As I passed through the room in which the baby had napped, I noticed one of my own blankets folded on the cedar chest at the foot of the bed. My voice in my mind said, "Put that blanket away." My immediate mental response was, "Well, not now, I will do it after the guests have gone. Right now the baby blanket is more important." But I am so used to following those hunches that I lifted my blanket to put it away. Under it was the baby blanket.

I have a very dear lifelong friend whose orthodox Christian background keeps her locked into certain terminology. She insists that all of her prayers for help must be directed to God. She is also convinced that it is the Holy Ghost who performs many of the miracles I talk about in parapsychology. I have no quarrel with this, for I believe we are on the same wavelength. She just prefers different terms that make her more comfortable. I often address my prayers to God, but I conceive of that supreme power as the Creative Source of all that is, totally loving, nonjudgmental and impartial. The spiritual hierarchy is part of the creation of that Source, and along with spirit entities, serves God or that Source by serving humanity.

It is remarkably easy to tap into this limitless source of information. Since almost everyone is already tuned in to the Source of their own being, the next step is to select the program you want to hear. It is quite similar to turning on a radio or a TV. All you get is noise and static until you select the station you want. Similarly, you can tune in to high-level intellects who will inspire you and guide you into activities that will enhance your experiences and bring you happiness; or you can tune in to undeveloped entities whose only desire is to express their own problems through human beings.

Never lose sight, however, of the fact that you cannot have the help of master guides until you qualify. Many people are very angry at God and complain that they have prayed and prayed and gone to church and given to charities, and still God is punishing them and not answering their prayers. Often when I talk with these people I can clearly hear by their conversation that they carry in their emotional nature resentments, anger, guilt, jealousy, arrogance, selfishness and other negative qualities that are tantamount to tuning in to the wrong department in the spiritual dimension. They are in constant conflict between what they are and what they want, and the sad fact is that they do not even know that they are creating their own blocks.

Once you understand the concept that your destiny is uniquely yours and exactly right for you because you have chosen it, there will be no room for recriminations in your thinking. You will look for the reasons for your experiences rather than blaming your parents, your siblings, your teachers, or God. Then you will be ready to flow in your own stream of consciousness, and you will be rewarded by an ever-increasing awareness of your connection with a benevolent power greater than yourself.

Summary

Are haunted houses a reality? Does possession really happen to people? Is channeling a possibility for everyone? The answer to every one of these questions is an undeniable affirmative. The fact that people question the existence of paranormal phenomena is not as surprising as the fact that, with so much incontrovertible evidence, observations of such incidents can be so summarily ignored or dismissed as groundless.

I have always had an insatiable drive to find answers to everything. I wanted to do things that others said could not be done, and discover the reasons for our sojourn on this planet. As a very young person I was angry at the injustice I observed all around me. My pious friends would often answer my inquiries with, "God's will be done." This comment impressed me as a totally inadequate explanation for life as I witnessed it. There had to be a better answer than that, and I spent a considerable amount of time looking for it. I recall a friend saying once, "I don't know why you have to go off on all of these tangents (referring to my interest in paranormal experiences). I just take it on faith." My reply was, "Fine, if that makes you happy, but I want to know what I have faith IN, and I think I have found it in this field."

Rather than taking away my Christian faith, studying the paranormal enhanced it. The beautiful precepts which Jesus gave us proved to be the same as the teachings of other great philosophical leaders throughout history. These time-honored precepts were

201

psychologically sound, and worked in a practical world. Discovering the philosophies of reincarnation and karma was a real breakthrough for me. If individuals are responsible for themselves, and literally create their own destiny through the exercise of free will, suffering for their mistakes and exercising their personal powers of determination to rectify their errors, then order and justice operate throughout the life experience.

Later I came to the conclusion that the philosophy of rebirth is limited to the physical world. Whenever individuals discovered that they were spirits with a body, rather than bodies with a spirit, they would recognize the love principle and transcend physical laws. Pain and discomfort become the tools we use to discover our true nature. Each individual soul is on a singular path to self-discovery, and each of us is responsible for finding that path. Humans as a species have been painfully slow about it. Legions of people are far from even possessing the ability to understand such a concept.

However, an advance toward living in harmony with spiritual principles is globally evident. Never at any time in our history have as many people been as concerned about as many other people as is true today. The changes in the international scene point to a concerted effort to solve disagreements with arbitration rather than swords or guns.

Over thirty years ago my search for knowledge led me into a direct encounter with reincarnation. While in a trance state, one of my clients spontaneously recalled a past-life experience that explained certain problems in her present life. When I found that all of my clients who could achieve an altered state and sincerely wanted answers to their problems were successful, and that dramatic changes occurred in their lives as a result, my own horizons widened immeasurably.

By its very nature, this discovery brought that other dimension into focus for me. It is a reality that dramatically changes our total perception of human beings, and our relationship to each other and to the planet we all inhabit. We are independent beings, yet dependent on each other as we interrelate to resolve problems and complete our own destinies. Discovering the reality of haunted houses and possession forced me to recognize that the interrelationship of lives and destinies was not confined to the earth experience, but extended into the spiritual dimension as well.

I must confess I have long resisted writing this book. Many volumes have already been published on the subject of haunts and possession. However, numerous people have urged me to share my own experiences and philosophy. A number of psychics have told me that they were impelled to advise me that I must do this, and my own sense of urgency about it finally got my full attention. My concern was: What can I add to the literature already in existence?

Many of the extant books are chronicles written for entertainment value. I wanted to write from the point-of-view of the spirit entities encountered. My primary purpose was to remove the tremendous fear of death that grips the human race, and to open the door to the realization that communication between the two dimensions is indeed a reality — a reality that has been in existence for centuries, yet is still unrecognized by most people.

However, I am reminded of the admonition of my orthodox friends who quote from the Bible: "Have nothing to do with familiar spirits." My answer to that advice is, "I could not agree with you more. Familiar spirits are the earthbound entities who cause immeasurable harm to the people who contact them." However, the Bible also states very clearly, "Test the spirits and see whether they be of God." These two statements speak clearly to all of the material in this book related to communication.

Case histories have been the primary source of presenting readers with the many facets and purposes of communication. In the first part of the book I described haunted houses, and some of the reasons why spirits, both benevolent and malevolent, remain earthbound. I also presented evidence of the ongoing life process on two planes.

The latter half of the book has focused primarily on invasion. Through numerous case histories we have explored the sorts of human problems that can be carried over into the other dimension following bodily death. Mediumship, now known as channeling, has a long history as a means of communication between the two dimensions. This phenomenon provides evidence for healthy and purposeful communication, as well as for painful, destructive interchanges.

I leave you, the reader, with a challenge. Test my hypothesis that there is purpose and design to human life, that this purpose can be known, and that cooperating with it can produce harmony and productive creativity in the life span of each individual on planet Earth.

Glossary

All-Knowing Mind — Human beings are more than physical organisms, and therefore know everything about the self at some higher level of the mind. It is this higher level of awareness that makes past-life therapy, and other therapies that access information from the past, so successful. By using an altered state of consciousness, or hypnosis, to communicate with the all-knowing mind, most people discover information about themselves of which they were totally unaware in their normal state of consciousness.

Astral Plane — A level of awareness in the etheric world having its own principles, inhabitants and reasons for being. It is like Earth's double, vibrating faster than the physical earth, but interpenetrating Earth to its core.

Astral Travel — A term used to describe soul travel, an experience in which the soul or spirit separates from the physical body and travels through space to unlimited distances. The spirit remains connected to the physical body by what is called the astral cord. Should this cord be broken, the body dies.

Aura — An electromagnetic, invisible but intelligent energy or force field surrounding an entity. In a healthy body the aura extends out from the body in thread-like emanations. Illness in the body is indicated by a drooping aura. The basic aura is white and extends out from the body about an inch or two. Beyond that the aura can expand to a number of feet and appear in multiple colors.

Automatic Writing — The practice of allowing an energy from the etheric dimension to control the hand and arm to write information that is often unknown to the individual.

Black Arts — The use of psychic energy to deliberately harm another person through the use of rituals and mind concentration.

Channeling — A term that has come into popularity in recent years and replaces the once-popular word "medium." A channel has the ability to allow an etheric world intelligence to impress his or her mind and convey messages of help and inspiration. At the present time many people claim to be channels in the fields of writing, lecturing, and research, and especially in conveying metaphysical information.

Charlatan — A quack; a person who pretends to have more knowledge than he or she actually possesses

Clairvoyance — "Clear vision;" the ability to see into the ethereal dimension without the use of the physical eyes. Reaching into another vibrational frequency and seeing "within the head".

Cuneiform — The wedge shaped writing of the ancient Persians, Babylonians and Assyrians.

Cyclotron —A powerful apparatus that sends out electrons at very high velocities. E. O. Lawrence was honored with a Nobel prize in physics in 1939 for his part in its development. His successful work resulted from a dream.

Ecumenical Conference — A meeting held by the Catholic church for the purpose of establishing and maintaining unity in the church, at which major decisions regarding theology and dogma are made. At one such conference in the 1550s, the belief in reincarnation was expunged from the tenets of the church, and the Apocryhpha removed from the Bible because it contained references to the belief in the rebirth of the soul.

Entity — In metaphysics this term refers to intelligent beings who no longer reside in a physical body. Entities can be seen by people who possess extended vision or clairvoyance. Entities are particularly famous for their help in providing information at seances. They are also credited with providing information to all individuals who are sensitive to their vibrations.

Exorcism — A ritual employed by priests or other trained individuals to remove offending spirits from people suffering from spirit attachments. The current term for this exercise is "spirit releasement." The term "spirit possession" has been used for centuries; "depossession" describes the removal of the malevolent spirits.

Force Field — An energy field generated within all living things; the infinite intelligence that permeates all life; the highest power in existence. Neutral in character, it takes on good or bad characteristics when utilized by the human mind.

Hallucinations — Objects and ideas having no basis in fact but accepted by the mind. Such thoughts or ideas are often triggered by delirium or drugs. Hallucinations are not to be confused with clairvoyant abilities, which enable some people to actually see and hear higher vibrations and be aware of realities in the ethereal dimension.

Hauntings — Any and all paranormal activities observed in buildings or in areas such as cemeteries. Hauntings, often referred to as poltergeist activities, can be caused by discarnate entities trapped for some reason in a specific location, or by the energy left at the conclusion of some very powerful traumatic event. Hauntings frequently appear to be intelligent spirits attempting to make contact with someone on the earth plane to convey a message.

Hydesville Knockings — The Fox sisters of Hydesville became the recipients of considerable ridicule and persecution because of their psychic ability. They held many seances in their home, which became known as the "Hydesville Knockings" because their questions were answered by knockings supposedly made by the invisible spirits.

Hypnotism — A method of preparing the conscious mind of an individual to relinquish conscious control and allow the subconscious mind to be in charge. Hypnotism may be used for therapeutic or harmful purposes.

Levitation — A state in which an object or person is elevated and remains momentarily suspended in mid-air. Levitation can be accomplished by individuals who have the mental power, or psychic ability, to interfere with the gravitational pull of the earth.

Malevolent Entities — Evil spirits who harass human beings, causing all manner of discomfort and distress. Strong evidence seems to support the hypothesis that these entities are often seeking revenge for some past injury.

Mediums — Individuals possessing a psychic gift which enables them to communicate with the dead. Mediums are most famous for holding seances at which the dead speak through them to contact loved ones, especially mourning relatives. In the trance state mediums allow their bodies to be totally taken over and controlled by the spirit, and retain no conscious knowledge of what they say or do. In recent years this phenomena has changed; many mediums now remain completely conscious of what they say and experience. The modern term for this experience is "channeling."

Mesmerism — An early form of hypnotism, named after Franz Anton Mesmer. Mesmer used hand passes, thought to convey a vital essence or fluid, to dominate the patient's will.

Metaphysics — Beyond earth physics, or invisible physics. A branch of philosophy that deals with first principles, an investigation into knowledge. A belief system that maintains that all things are a part of a single source.

Multiple Personality — The term applied to persons who have literally more than one personality, each separate and unaware of the others. Some people can switch from one personality to another in minutes. Each personality has its own body chemistry, characteristics, talents and capabilities.

Obsession — A condition in which an inferior etheric world entity is able to psychically transfer its thoughts and feelings to a living human being. The problem may endure over a long period of time. The recipient of the entitiy's thoughts responds to its negativity and depression without realizing that these feelings are being imposed from the outside. Obsession is not to be confused with possession.

Ouija Board — A board on which are printed the alphabet, numbers, and the words "yes" and "no." In the hands of a psychic the planchet (a pointer) moves over the board to spell out answers to questions. The ouija board can be a dangerous tool in the hands of persons inexperienced in the psychic sciences.

Paranormal Phenomena — Experiences outside of the accepted models of science. Paranormal phenomena include many manifestations of psychic gifts: clairvoyance, telepathy, psychometry, telekinesis, hauntings, and any other phenomena that cannot be explained by the five senses.

Past-Life Therapy, or **Past-life Regression Therapy** — A technique used to assist individuals into an altered state of consciousness or a trance state for the purpose of exploring the subconscious mind. It is a highly successful tool for recovering buried trauma and events from the past that interfere with an individual's ability to function normally in the present. Irrational fears, phobias, and compulsive behaviors can be brought into the conscious mind and reintegrated with the present personality, relieving the symptoms. The term implies reincarnation, but such a belief is not a prerequisite for success with this technique.

Poltergeist — A "mischievous spirit;" a discarnate entity who enjoys playing pranks on humans. Poltergeist energy apparently derives from humans who are disturbed or angry, especially young people; the activity only occurs in the presence of these people. Poltergeists can be benevolent or malevolent; most enjoy moving furniture, displacing objects, and making a lot of noise.

Possession — A compulsive invasion of a living organism by a low-grade spirit entity. The evil-intentioned entity acts from within the borrowed body, substituting its own will and intention for the duration of the seizure. A new personality may appear which is totally foreign to that of the host personality. In a process now called releasement, the invading entity can be expelled and sent into the light. Such experiences can last over a considerable period of time, and are sometimes difficult to resolve. It is important to note that the personality of the victim is in large measure responsible for the invasion. Discarnate entities who are angry, vindictive, and/or resentful are attracted to people who harbor those same emotions.

Psychic — Any individual who is sensitive to phenomena beyond the five senses and aware of activity in the ethereal dimension. Psychics can often see spirit forms, hear spirit voices, and "know" events that are going to happen in the future. They are often uncomfortable because they are aware of the vibrations of the people around them. Many people are born with this ability; it can also be developed with intention and practice. It is important to recognize the difference between this natural gift and mental illness.

Reincarnation — The philosophical belief that the soul is infinite, and on a spiritual journey to achieve perfection. In order to reach this perfect state, the soul must experience many physical incarnations, each one enabling the soul to learn spiritual lessons and come closer to the goal of perfection. The soul chooses every experience for the lesson it contains. Each problem, if it is handled with positive energy, provides an opportunity to make soul progress. The concept of reincarnation incorporates the major teachings of Jesus, such as unconditional love and service to others.

Seance — Sometimes called a "sitting," a seance consists of a group of people meeting with a medium or channel to attempt to contact dead relatives or loved ones. Seances began in the United States in the mid-1800s when the two Fox sisters became the targets of spirits from the other side. For a number of years the spirits sent messages to many people who sought contact with a dead loved one. Seances are still common. Unlike earlier mediums, today's channel does not always go into a complete trance, but remains aware of the message coming through her/him.

Spirit Guide — Many people believe that they have a spirit guide or guardian angel. This celestial being accompanies and assists a person in various ways. For most people this help appears as a hunch or a subtle feeling that comes over them. Other individuals claim to be in conscious contact with their guides at all times. Volumes have been written delineating case histories of people whose lives have benefited from this kind of intervention.

Spiritualism — This belief system teaches that all who die enter an ethereal realm, where they live in spirit form and are able to communicate with their living loved ones and friends. Spiritualism is a religious philosophy; the tenets of the church are very similar to Christian ethics, and teach the value of love and good works. Spiritualism is not the same as "spiritism," as taught by Allen Kardec, who believed in spirit survival but was opposed to treating the philosophy as a religion.

Table-tipping — A method of communication with the spirit world. Any size table will respond. In table-tipping, a number of people sit around a table. Each person touches the table very lightly with all five fingers. In unison the group chants, "table up, table up." An immediate response often follows. The table may quiver, or lift on one side. If someone in the group possesses powerful energy the table may lift off the floor or rock back and forth. The group then asks questions, which are answered by the table tapping the floor once or twice to indicate "yes" or "no." If a skeptic is present the table generally will not respond. Table-tipping is used as a parlor game by many, but it can be dangerous. Very unpleasant entities may be contacted if the group is not protected by positive energy.

Telepathy — Mind-to-mind communication. Many years of research were carried out by Dr. Rhine at Duke University and the results were declared incontrovertible. He proved that the mind could communicate with other minds and successfully transmit specific information.

Thought Forms — There is much evidence that a person's thoughts create specific forms which can be seen by psychics. Happy thoughts create beautiful forms in pleasant colors. Ugly, angry thoughts create muddy, red forms in ugly shapes, often with hooks. C. W. Leadbeater has made several excellent studies of this phenomena.

Typology — Another term for "table-tipping." See above.

Bibliography

Bayless, Raymond. *The Enigma of the Poltergeist*. New York: Parker Publishing Co., 1967.

Blatty, William Peter. *The Exorcist*. New York: Harper & Row, Publishers, 1971.

Brian, Dent. *Jeane Dixon: The Witnesses*. New York: Warner Books, 1976.

Brown, Rosemary. *Unfinished Symphonies*. New York: William Morrow and Co. Inc., 1971.

Capra, Frijof. *The Tao of Physics*. Berkeley, CA: Shambhala Publishers, 1975.

Chaplin, Annabel. *The Bright Light of Death*. Marina Del Rey, CA. DeVorss & Co., 1977.

Crookall, Robert. *During Sleep*. Secaucus, NJ: University Books, Inc., 1974.

Daily, Starr. *Well Springs of Immortality*. St. Paul: Macalester Park Publishing Co., 1941.

Doyle, Sir Arthur Conan. *The Edge of the Unknown*. New York: G. P. Putnams Sons, 1930.

Denning, Melita, and Osborne Phillips. *Psychic Self-defense and Well Being*. St. Paul: Llewellyn Publications, 1984.

Ebon, Martin. *Exorcism.* New York: The New American Library, Inc., 1974.

_____. *The Devil's Bride, Exorcism: Past & Present.* New York: Harper & Row, Publishers, 1974.

_____. *They Knew the Unknown.* New York: The World Publishing Co., 1971.

Edwards, Frank. *Strange World.* New York: Lyle Stuart, Inc., 1964.

Ferguson, Marilyn. *The Aquarian Conspiracy.* Los Angeles: J. P. Tarcher, Inc., 1980.

Fortune, Dion. *Psychic Self Defense.* Hackensack, NJ: Wehman Bros., 1971.

Gruzdis, Robert L. *The Common-Sense Approach to Ghosts.* Buffalo Grove, IL: Knowledge Unlimited, 1986.

Hall, Manly P. *Reincarnation, The Cycle of Necessity.* Los Angeles: The Philosophical Research Society, Inc. 1967.

Hardinge, Emma. *Modern American Spiritualism.* London: Progressive Library & Spiritual Institution, 1869.

Harman, Willis, Ph.D. and Howard Rheingold. *Higher Creativity.* Los Angeles: Jeremy P. Tarcher, Inc., 1984.

Heron, Lawrence Tunstall. *ESP in the Bible.* Garden City, NY: Doubleday and Co., Inc., 1974.

House, Brant, Editor. *Strange Powers of Unusual People.* New York: Ace Books, Inc., 1963.

Hurwood, Bernhardt J. *Vampires, Werewolves, and Ghouls.* New York: Ace Books, Inc., 1968.

Keene, M. Lamar. *Psychic Mafia.* New York: Dell Publishing Co., 1976.

Klimo, Jon. *Channeling.* Los Angeles: Jeremy P. Tarcher, 1987.

Leadbeater, C. W. *The Other Side of Death.* Adyar, Madras, India: The Theosophical Publishing House, 1954.

_____, and Annie Besant. *Thought Forms.* Wheaton, IL: The Theosophical Publishing House, 1925.

Leak, Sybil. *Diary of a Witch.* New York: A Signet Book, 1968.

LeShan, Lawrence. *The Medium, The Mystic, and The Physicist.* New York: The Viking Press, 1974.

Logan, Daniel. *The Reluctant Prophet.* Garden City, NY: Doubleday and Co. Inc., 1968.

Lucas, Winafred Blake, Ph.D. *Regression Therapy, Handbook for Professionals.* Crest Park, CA: Deep Forest Press, 1993.

Manning, Matthew. *The Link.* New York: Holt, Rhinehart & Winston, 1975.

Millard, Joseph. *Edgar Cayce, Mystery Man of Miracles.* Greenwich, CT: Fawcett Publications, Inc., 1967.

Montandon, Pat. *The Intruders.* New York: Coward, McCann & Geoghegan, Inc., 1975.

Nassau, E. *How to Combat Psychic Attack.* Prescott, AZ: E. Nassau, 1957.

Oesterreich, T. K. *Possession.* New Hyde Park, NY: University Books, 1966.

Schreiber, Flora Rheba. *Sybil.* New York: Warner Books, Inc., 1974.

Shirley, Ralph. *Occultists and Mystics of All Ages.* New Hyde Park, NY: University Books Inc., 1972

Spraggett, Allen. *The Unexplained.* New York: The New American Library, 1967.

St. Clair, David. *Psychic Healers.* Garden City, NY: Doubleday and Co., Inc., 1974.

Stearns, Jess. *Edgar Cayce, The Sleeping Prophet.* Garden City, NY: Doubleday and Co., Inc., 1967

Sugerman, A. Arthur and Ralph E. Tarter. Editors. *Expanding Dimensions of Consciousness.* New York: Springer Publishing Co., 1978.

Sugrue, Thomas. *Edgar Cayce.* New York: Dell Publishing Co., Inc., 1945.

Van Dusen, Wilson. *The Presence of Spirits in Madness.* New York: The Swedenborg Foundation, Inc., 1978.

Walker, Danton. *I Believe In Ghosts*. New York: Taplinger
Publishing Co., 1969.

Weiss, Brian L., M.D. *Many Lives, Many Masters*. New York: Simon &
Schuster, Inc., 1988.

Wickland, Carl A., M.D. *Thirty Years Among The Dead*. Amherst, WI:
Amherst Press, 1924. Reprint, Las Vegas, NV: Health Research,
1971.

Woolger, Roger J. *Other Lives, Other Selves*. New York: Doubleday
and Co., Inc., 1987.

Young, Alan. *Spiritual Healing*. Marina Del Rey, CA: DeVorss & Co.,
1981.

Index

About the Author

As a small child, Hazel Denning had an insatiable desire to know the reason for everything, and her search for truth began early in life. In her twenties she began teaching and lecturing. For the past sixty-five years she has devoted the major part of her time to investigating paranormal phenomena. For twelve years, with the assistance of two remarkably gifted psychics, she investigated haunted houses and cases of possession.

She studied under eminent scholars in extension courses and workshops, eventually entering the university and earning two Master's degrees and a Ph.D. in Clinical Psychology. She also earned a doctorate in metaphysical counseling. For thirty-seven years she has had a full-time career as a Past-Life Regression Therapist.

The author has appeared on numerous TV programs, been interviewed by Oprah Winfrey and Tom Snyder, and lectured in Japan, England, Holland, India, Brazil, and the United States. She is currently an instructor with the Professional Institute for Regression Therapy. She has been quoted in many books, is the author of a monograph and many articles, and is one of the authors of *Regression Therapy, A Handbook for Professionals*.

164   (186)